D1570610

CONCURRENT PROGRAMMING

CONCURRENT PROGRAMMING

ILLUSTRATED WITH EXAMPLES IN PORTAL,
MODULA-2 AND ADA

André Schiper

Translated by Jack Howlett

Halsted Press: a division of
John Wiley & Sons Inc. New York

English translation © North Oxford Academic Publishers Ltd, 1989

Original French language edition (Programmation concurrente)
published by Presses Polytechniques Romandes, Lausanne
© Presses Polytechniques Romandes, 1986

English edition first published in 1989 by North Oxford Academic Publishers Ltd,
a subsidiary of Kogan Page Ltd, 120 Pentonville Road, London N1 9JN

Published in the USA by Halsted Press:
a division of John Wiley & Sons Inc. New York

Library of Congress Cataloging-in-Publication Data
Schiper, André.
  Concurrent programming/André Schiper.
    p. cm.
  "A Halsted Press book."
  Bibliography: p.
  Includes index.
  ISBN 0-470-21346-9 : $34.95
  1. Parallel programming (Computer science) I. Title.
QA76.6.S385   1988
004'.35—dc19   88-32709

Printed and bound in Great Britain

Ada is a registered trademark of the United States Government (Ada Joint Program Office).

PDP is a trademark of Digital Equipment Corporation.

CONTENTS

To Françoise, Isabelle and Nicolas

FOREWORD

Traditionally, teaching of concurrent programming has been confined to courses on operating systems. The reasons are historical: for a long time operating systems have been the favoured field for the application of concurrent programming and the drivers of its development. But things are now changing: on the one hand the subject is slowly reaching maturity, on the other its techniques are no longer used exclusively for writing operating systems – to give just one example, they are now applied to problems of industrial control.

These considerations, together with the appearance of languages such as Portal, Modula-2 and Ada, have stimulated us to write a book devoted to concurrent programming.

Chapter 1

INTRODUCTION

This chapter defines concurrent programming and gives short accounts of the programming languages Portal, Modula-2 and Ada.

1.1 CONCURRENT PROGRAMMING: DEFINITION

A concurrent program is a program that is not sequential. This is not a definition that explains very much, so to make matters clearer let us consider the evaluation of the simple expression (a + b)*(c + d). A *sequential* evaluation consists of computing first (a + b), then (c + d), and finally the product of these sums; in a *concurrent* evaluation (a + b) and (c + d) are computed *simultaneously*, and then the product.

The advantage of concurrent evaluation is clear if we have two (or in general more) processors, for then one can be evaluating (a + b) while the other is evaluating (c + d), and the total time needed to compute the product is reduced. But suppose we have only one – do we gain any advantage? We can interpret 'concurrent' evaluation in this way: the processor works for a small fraction of a second on the computation of (a + b), then for the same (very short) length of time on (c + d), then switches back to (a + b) for the same short time, and so on until both sums have been computed. Does this bring any advantage? The answer is no. Nevertheless, concurrent programming is an important technique even in the case of a single processor. To see why this is so we will next consider the handling of input and output, for here concurrent programming enables us to exploit to the full the possibilities for parallel operation of the processor and the peripheral units.

Consider the problem of writing characters on the screen of a terminal. Figure 1.1 shows the activities of the processor and the interface to the screen, respectively:

- first, the processor waits until the peripheral interface is ready to accept a character (it can be informed of this by an interrupt signal); when it knows that the interface is ready to receive, it sends the character that is to be written;
- the interface waits until the character has been received, then transfers it to the screen and finally informs the processor (for example, by means of another interrupt) that the writing action has been completed.

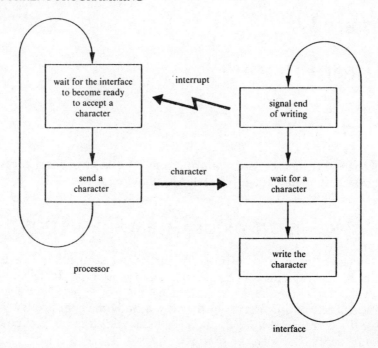

Figure 1.1 **Writing to the screen: actions of the processor and of the screen interface.**
Initially, the interface is waiting for a character.

It would seem from Figure 1.1 that the processor must remain idle while waiting for the interface to become ready to accept a character; but this is not necessarily so, and can be avoided by simply providing it with work to do. This desire to avoid idling has led to the idea of concurrent programming.

Let us illustrate concurrency of processing with input/output by considering the running of a small sawmill in which a single operator receives and carries out customers' orders. We can equate the operator's activities with the execution of a program on a single processor. The workshop has two 'input devices':

- a telephone, over which the customers send orders;
- a window at which customers can queue in order to give in orders.

There is also an 'output device', a conveyor belt on which the operator places the wood he has cut to the dimensions required in the order (we are not concerned with how this finally gets to the customer).

Suppose now that the telephone has no bell and there is no buzzer or other means of summoning attention at the window. The activity in the workshop corresponds to the execution of the following program:

- the operator waits for an order to arrive, alternating between picking up the telephone (to find if there is a customer on the line) and going to the window (to see if there is a customer waiting);

- when he receives an order (by either route) he carries it out; that is, he cuts the specified wood to the specified dimensions;
- when he has finished, he tries to place the wood he has just cut on the conveyor. He may not be able to do so because the conveyor is still loaded with the previous order, in which case he waits until it becomes free; this is the comparison with the waiting of the processor in Figure 1.1.

This is a sequential operation of the sawmill. We can change to a concurrent operation by introducing bells as follows:

- a telephone bell;
- a bell at the window, for the customer to call the operator's attention;
- a bell associated with the conveyor, to let the operator know that there is room for another load.

These equate to the interrupt signals previously mentioned. They lead to a different way of organizing the work in which there are:

- a file of orders;
- a shelf on which the wood is placed after cutting.

The operator now goes about his work as follows. He looks at the file of orders, takes the earliest of these, carries it out and puts the wood either on the shelf or directly on the conveyor if it is free. However, any of the bells may ring, and if this happens he interrupts whatever he is doing at that instant (to resume it later):

- if it is either the telephone or the bell at the window he enters the new order in his file;
- if it is the conveyor he takes wood from the shelf and puts it on the belt.

This is a more efficient way of working than the first, because:

- the workman does not have to wait, unoccupied, for the conveyor to become free, so he does more work in the day;
- the customers do not have to wait, impatiently, on the telephone or at the window; orders are taken as they arrive and not, as before, at the rate at which they can be dealth with.

Even this improvement, however, would not necessarily correspond to the most efficient form of concurrent programming. The approach has the disadvantage that the complexity of the corresponding program increases greatly as the number of peripherals increases. Taking the workshop again, a better use of time would be achieved if three further employees were added, one at the window, the telephone and the conveyor respectively. The first would enter each new order in the file as it was received from the newly-arrived customer, the second would do the same for telephoned orders and the third would load wood on to the conveyor whenever the bell rang to indicate that this was free. The mill operator would continue as before except that:

- he would not need to attend either to the telephone or to the counter, but only to look in the file for orders;
- he would always put the wood he had just cut on the shelf, never on the conveyor.

In the terminology of concurrent programming the operator and the three assistants would be called processes. This idea of a process enables us to deal with the complexity of a program that manages a number of peripherals. It is clear that if there is only a single processor only one process can be in execution at any one time. In the workshop analogy, this means that only one of the four people can be in action at any one time, so that, for example:

- when a bell rings the person p1 who is active at that instant stops and the person p2 who should respond to that ring goes into action;
- when p2 has completed his task he becomes inactive and p1 resumes.

This does not affect the operation of the workshop. But now suppose we take a film of it at work: if we run this through a projector at high speed we shall get the impression that all four people are working simultaneously all the time. More important, since an interrupt (a bell ringing) can occur at any instant we have to imagine, in considering a concurrent program, that the different processes are all executing simultaneously.

1.2   SYNCHRONIZATION AND MUTUAL EXCLUSION

The concurrent organization of the workshop raises two problems, those of *mutual exclusion* and *synchronization* respectively: these are problems common to all concurrent programs.

Mutual exclusion can be illustrated by considering the workshop's file of orders. Suppose that while the assistant at the window is entering an order the telephone rings. If the telephone assistant can take over the file immediately and enter his order, there is a risk of meaningless entries being made. One has therefore to prevent the file from being removed while an order is being entered. An alternative would be to write each new order on a separate sheet and to give these to the mill operator separately: this does not remove the risk but only transfers it (the need now is to prevent the two assistants from attempting to take the same sheet).

For the synchronization problem, consider the actions of the operator. He must stop working when he has no more orders (or when the shelf is full) and start again when he receives a new order (or when space becomes free on the shelf). In its general form the synchronization problem arises whenever several processes are involved in a cycle of activity. In the case of the workshop, this cycle comprises the assistants at the window and the telephone, the operator and finally the assistant at the conveyor.

These two types of problems are dealt with using tools or mechanisms called *locks, events, semaphores, monitors* and *rendezvous* respectively, which are described in Chapters 4 and 5. The list is not exhaustive but is a representative selection of the tools of concurrent programming:

- the lock is the simplest tool imaginable;
- the event is very simple and very widely used: it is found in many operating systems;
- the semaphore is a classical tool: it enables simple problems to be solved and is easy to implement;
- the monitor and the rendezvous are powerful modern tools.

The exercises given at the end of each chapter provide an opportunity for the reader to compare these different mechanisms.

1.3   CONCURRENT AND REAL-TIME PROGRAMMING

Concurrent programming cannot be discussed without making some reference to real-time programming, for the two concepts are related:

- as does a concurrent program, a real-time program manages peripherals;
- real-time programming uses the techniques of concurrent programming.

A real-time program further comprises another aspect, that of controlling some external system [Computer 84, Spector 84] which imposes time constraints on the program. A few examples are:

- industrial robots
- domestic central heating systems
- telephone exchanges
- control of laboratory experiments
- automatic flight navigation.

Consider for example the control of a central heating system. The input devices are the room temperature recorders, the output devices are the power-operated valves that turn the radiators on or off. The requirement on the control might be to keep the rooms at 20°C by day and 16°C by night. To achieve this the program must react in 'real time' (meaning within a time that must not exceed a stated maximum) to any observed temperature change, sending the appropriate instructions to the control valves. This sums up the features common to all real-time programs:

- the program receives information from the external system that it is controlling;
- it processes this information;
- it reacts by sending appropriate commands to the external system.

1.4 THE LANGUAGES PORTAL, MODULA-2 AND ADA

Concurrent and real-time programs can be written entirely in any of these modern languages. This has not always been possible. For a long time real-time programming was a matter of using multi-task operating systems that made suitable tools (in particular, for synchronization) available to application programs. These were written either in assembly language or in a higher level language that included calls to the operating system (for example Coral 66 [Woodward 70] or RTL/2 [Barnes 76]). Languages that included the concepts of concurrency began to appear during the first half of the 1970s, among which were PEARL [Werum 83] and Concurrent Pascal [Brinch Hansen 75]. Portal, Modula-2 and Ada are more recent, which is one reason for choosing them here; another is that they represent the present state of the art in this field. Finally because these languages take three different points of view in approaching the problem their study gives a more complete picture of the subject.

The Portal language [Businger 86] was defined by the Landis & Gyr company in 1978; its characteristic feature is the use of the concept of monitor for handling concurrency. We give an account of the language in Chapter 6, in which we explain in detail the semantics of monitors and illustrate one possible implementation.

The Modula-2 language [Wirth 85] was designed by Niklaus Wirth, the author of Pascal, in 1980. It must not be confused with the earlier language Modula, also due to Wirth [Wirth 77] which, like Portal, made use of the monitor concept. Wirth was led to design Modula-2 after experimenting with Modula; the new language embodies an original approach to real-time programming, having no built-in synchronization mechanism but offering the user the means for constructing one for himself.

The Ada language [DoD 83] is the culmination of a project initiated by the US Department of Defense in 1975, with the goal of developing a single language that would be adapted to all their applications. The specifications of the language were published in 1977 and 17 proposals were received, from Europe and the USA. Of these, four were short-listed and in 1979 the final choice was given to the language developed at CII-Honeywell-Bull by a team lead by J. Ichbiah. This language was christened Ada – after Augusta Ada, Countess of Lovelace, who worked with Babbage in 1830–1840 – and was standardized by ANSI in 1983. Its characteristic feature is the use of the rendezvous concept. Later it will be interesting to use the same synchronization problem to compare the concepts of Portal (monitor) and Ada (rendezvous).

We must emphasize that this book does not aim to be a reference manual for these three languages. Its aim is to show the reader how to solve the problems of current programming and to use judiciously the mechanisms they provide. The sequential features of the languages are not treated, but the reader who knows Pascal will have no difficulty in following the texts of the algorithms; in fact, we have taken care to make these as easily comprehensible as possible. Nevertheless, we suggest that the reader assimilates Appendix 1 before starting on the rest of the book.

Chapter 2

INPUT/OUTPUT AND INTERRUPTS

Concurrent programming is closely linked with the handling of input/ output peripherals, so it is important to start by considering the underlying principles. We shall consider the case of the PDP-11 machine, which has the advantage of being particularly simple.

2.1   ARCHITECTURE OF THE PDP-11

Figure 2.1 illustrates the architecture of the PDP-11 [DEC 83], showing the bus, the processor, the main memory (of 16-bit words) and an interface to a terminal (only one interface is shown, but there can be several). Information can flow via the bus between the processor, the memory and the interfaces. The terminal interface has four registers which are involved in the programming of input and output; we will discuss these further below. Meanwhile it is important to note that these registers are accessed by the processor as though they were locations in the memory (the addresses are given in the next paragraph). Figure 2.1 also shows two important registers in the processor:

- the processor status word (psw);
- the program counter (pc).

At any instant the program counter contains the address in main memory of the instruction to be executed next. Three bits in the processor status word define the processor's priority, which can therefore have any of the eight values 0 to 7 (see Figure 2.2). We shall see in §2.3 how this priority is used in handling interrupts.

2.2   BUSY WAITING INPUT/OUTPUT

Let us consider the very simple case of programming a terminal interface. Notice first that a terminal really consists of two completely distinct peripherals – a keyboard and a screen – which are programmed independently.

We start with writing to the screen. This uses the two last registers shown in Figure 2.1:

- the register giving the state of the screen. The standard address of this register is 177564 (octal) (see Figure 2.3);
- the screen data register, with standard octal address 177566 (see Figure 2.4).

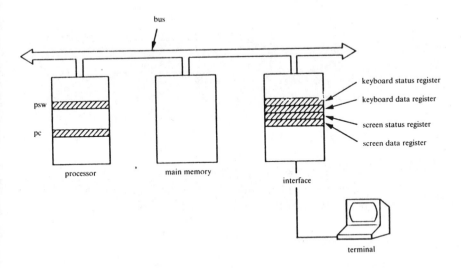

Figure 2.1   Architecture of the PDP-11

When a character is to be written to the screen the system must first wait until the interface is ready to receive it: it will not be ready if the transfer of the previous character is not complete. The interface signals its readiness by setting bit 7 of the status register to 1. Then all that has to be done is to put the ASCII code for the character in the screen data register: the interface will make the transfer and clear bit 7 ready for the next transfer. We can write the procedure as follows (where we have used mem[adr].word to denote the

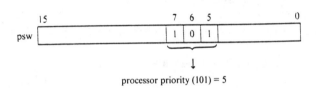

processor priority (101) = 5

Figure 2.2   Processor status word

19

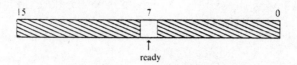

Figure 2.3 Screen status register

Figure 2.4 Screen data register

contents of the word corresponding to memory address adr, and mem[adr].bit[i] for the content of bit number i in this word):

```
procedure write(c: char);

  const
    screen_status = 177564B;
      (* octal address of screen status register *)
    screen_data   = 177566B;
      (* octal address of screen data register *)
    ready = 7; (* bit number *)

  code
    while mem[screen_status].bit[ready] = 0 do (* wait *)
    end while;
    mem[screen_data].word: = c (* writing *)
  end write;
```

A similar procedure reads a character typed on the keyboard, using two other registers shown in Figure 2.1:

- the keyboard status register, with standard octal address 177560 (Figure 2.5);
- the keyboard data register, with standard octal address 177562 (Figure 2.6).

Bit 7 in the status register is set to indicate that the data register contains a

20

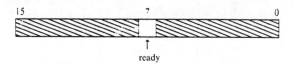

Figure 2.5   Keyboard status register

Figure 2.6   Keyboard data register

character; after it has been read this bit is automatically cleared. The read procedure is as follows:

```
procedure read (var c: char);

   const
      keyboard_status = 177560B;
         (* octal address of keyboard status register *)
      keyboard_data = 1775621B;
         (* octal address of keyboard data register *)
      ready = 7; (* bit number *)

code
   while mem[keyboard_status].bit[ready] = 0 do (* wait *)
   end while;
   c: = mem[keyboard_data].word (* reading *)
end read;
```

As we have said, the terminal keyboard and screen are two distinct peripherals, and therefore a procedure must be provided to write on the screen a character read from the keyboard; this is called *echoing a character*:

```
procedure read_with_echo (var c: char);
code
   read(c);   (* above procedure *)
   write (c); (* above procedure *)
end read_with_echo;
```

21

2.3 INTERRUPT-DRIVEN INPUT/OUTPUT

If input/output is programmed in the way just given, the processor will spend most of its time waiting for bit 7 of the status register to be set. Thus with a screen speed of 2400 bauds (240 characters per second) it will spend about 99 per cent of its time testing this bit in the screen register. This is tolerable if there is only one terminal to be served and not a great deal of computing to be done, but not if the single processor has to manage several terminals and also provide a computing service to several users (as in a time-sharing system). In this case I/O must be handled using the *interrupt mode*, in which the processor is relieved of the burden of testing bit 7.

Taking again the case of writing to the screen, interrupt mode is enabled by setting bit 6 of the screen status register (Figure 2.7).

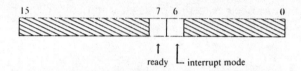

Figure 2.7   Screen status register

In this mode an interrupt is generated either whenever bit 7 changes from 0 to 1, or when bit 6 changes from 0 to 1 and bit 7 is already set. The latter means that the interface is already in a state ready to receive when the interrupt mode is enabled. An interrupt can be regarded as a procedure call initiated by some event external to the processor.

All the information that the processor needs in order to handle the interrupt is held in a pair of consecutive words called an *interrupt vector*. Each interrupt source has its own interrupt vector located at a fixed address. An interrupt vector contains the following information:

- the address of the procedure to be called in response to the interrupt – that is, a new value to be put into the program counter (pc);
- the new value to be put in the processor status register psw, which will define the processor's priority during the handling of the interrupt. We shall see the reason for this later.

When an interrupt occurs the processor saves the contents of pc and psw on a stack and loads these registers with the values in the vector corresponding to the interrupt. The effect of this is to:

- change the processor priority;
- start the execution of the procedure handling the interrupt.

After the interrupt has been treated, the pc and psw registers are restored to

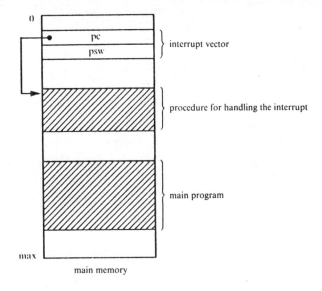

Figure 2.8 Interrupt vector

their original values, popped from the stack, with the result that:

- the processor returns to its previous priority;
- the statement sequence continues from the point where it was interrupted.

The change of processor priority during the interrupt handling is most important: it enables any further interrupt from the same peripheral to be temporarily masked, thus avoiding any possibility of error arising from two or more simultaneous executions of the same interrupt procedure. This masking depends on processor and interrupt priorities. Each interrupt source is given its own fixed priority – for example, 4 for the screen or keyboard. When the processor is at priority p all interrupts of priority equal to or less than p are inhibited: an interrupt of priority $q \leqslant p$ will not be dealt with until the processor priority has been reduced to a value below q. Thus the procedure called in response to an interrupt should be executed at a priority equal to that of the interrupt.

The text of Figure 2.9 illustrates the principle of writing a complete line to the screen in interrupt mode. Recall that the screen interrupt vector is stored at octal 64 and that in the PDP-11 addresses a and a+2 refer to consecutive words. The example of Figure 2.9 is given in the form of a module (see Appendix 1) that exports the procedure write_line. This procedure copies the parameters fline, flength into the variables line, length, local to the module, and then enables interrupt mode by initialising the interrupt vector and

23

```
const n = 80;
type tline = array 1 . . n of char;

module screen;
defines write_line; (* procedure exported from module *)

  const
    screen_vector = 64B; (* address of interrupt vector *)
    screen_status = 177564B; (* address of screen status register *)
    screen_data   = 177566B; (* address of screen data register *)
    inter_mode    = 6; (* no of bit *)

  var
    line:   tline;    (* line to be written *)
    length: integer; (* length of line *)
    i:      integer; (* index of next character in the line to be written *)

procedure write_line (fline:tline; flength:integer);
(* initialize writing in interrupt mode fline[1] to fline[length] *)
code
    line: = fline; length: = flength;
    i: = 1;
    mem[screen_vector].word: = address of procedure "interrupt";
              (* pc for interrupt *)
    mem[screen_vector + 2].word: = priority 4;
              (* psw for execution of procedure "interrupt"
                (interruption of priority 4) *)
    mem[screen_status].bit[inter_mode]: = 1
              (* enable interrupt mode *)
end write_line;

procedure interrupt;
(* called at each interrupt, writes the character line[i] *)
code
    mem[screen_data].word: = line[i];
    i: = i + 1;
    if i > length then mem[screen_status].bit[inter_mode]: = 0
        (* line complete; disable interrupt mode *)
    end if;
    restore values of pc, psw saved on stack (* return to main program *)
end interrupt;

end screen;
```

Figure 2.9 Writing a line to the screen in interrupt mode

setting bit 6 in the screen status register. The interrupt procedure then responds to each successive interrupt by writing the character line[i] to the screen and incrementing i, the complete line having been written when i > length. The timing of the operation is shown in Figure 2.10:

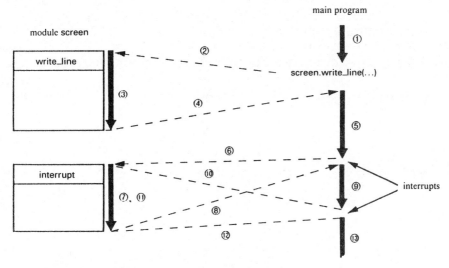

Figure 2.10   Timing of example of Figure 2.9

- the main program starts by calling procedure write_line of module screen. After this it continues execution without taking any part in writing;
- when interrupts occur they are treated by the interrupt procedure, the main program being unaware of it. Thus the writing to the screen takes place in parallel with the execution of the main program.

Consider now the case of reading characters from the keyboard: interrupt mode is enabled by setting bit 6 in the keyboard status register, the interrupt vector is at octal address 60 and the priority is again 4. We shall not consider reading further here, but we shall return to the subject later, particularly in Chapter 6 when we have developed adequate tools for a more complete treatment of input/output in interrupt mode.

2.4   DIRECT MEMORY ACCESS (DMA) INPUT/OUTPUT

The terminal interface just described requires action by the processor for every character input or output. This is not too serious a burden in the case of a terminal which is a relatively slow peripheral, but would be intolerable in the case of a disc (the transfer of one word or byte would scarcely have been completed before the next presented itself). The type of interface used then is one that can transfer a complete block of words. It is called a Direct Memory Access (DMA) interface and typically involves four registers to specify:

- a disc address
- a main memory address
- a number of words to be transferred
- the direction of transfer (disc to memory or memory to disc).

The interrupt is raised when the DMA interface has completed the transfer.

Chapter 3

THE PROCESS CONCEPT

We saw in Chapter 2 how the programming of input/output results in activities that make intermittent use of the processor. The process is a tool for handling such a situation.

3.1   MOTIVATION

Consider a time-sharing operating system whose aim is to provide a fair service (we define this term later) to each of the users working at terminals connected to the system. Figure 3.1 shows a typical configuration. For simplicity we shall consider only the terminals, ignoring the disc and the printer. The system has to read commands typed by each user, execute them

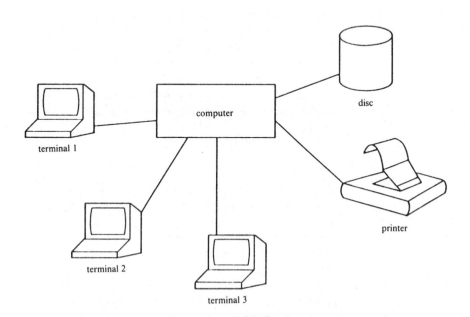

Figure 3.1   Typical time-sharing system

and return the results to the originating terminal. This can be expressed as follows for each terminal:

```
procedure serve_terminal(no: integer); (* serve terminal number no *)
code
    read a command from terminal no;
    execute this command;
    return results to terminal no;
end serve_terminal;
```

One way to express the time-sharing would be as follows (restricted to three terminals):

```
program time_sharing_system;
code
  loop
    serve_terminal(1);
    serve_terminal(2);
    serve_terminal(3);
  end loop
end time_sharing_system;
```

This would not be very satisfactory for several reasons:

- the inputs and outputs can only be expressed using busy waiting; this is inefficient since the time spent waiting for a character from terminal 1 could be used to execute a command from terminal 2;
- it does not take into account the possibility of different execution times for different commands, which is equivalent to inequitable treatment of the different terminals;
- it does not take into account the possibility of the different users working at different speeds.

These advantages are avoided if the inputs and outputs are handled in interrupt mode, but the expression given is not adapted to this. The form is sequential, which an interrupt handling program is not: when interrupt mode is enabled the processor either executes a command from one of the terminals or, intermittently, deals with input or output. The difficulty can be overcome with the process concept. A process can be regarded as a sequential program that executes instructions one after the other, and the juxtaposition of several processes will allow the expression of a non-sequential task. Thus, for the above example, we define a process for each terminal as follows:

```
process terminal1;    (* serve terminal number 1 *)
code
  loop
    serve_terminal(1) (* above procedure *)
  end loop
end terminal1;

process terminal2;    (* serve terminal number 2 *)
code
  loop
    serve_terminal(2)
  end loop
end terminal2;

process terminal3;    (* serve terminal number 3 *)
code
  loop
    serve_terminal(3)
  end loop
end terminal3;
```

The difference between the two expressions is greater than might be thought at first sight. In the second, each process has only one part of the original problem to deal with, so that the solution of a non-sequential problem has been reduced to that of a set of sequential problems. The seeming conjuring trick is made possible by what is called a *kernel*, which implements the process concept (see §3.3). Of course, if there is only one processor then only one process can be executed at any one time; but if each process is executed in turn for a short enough time the impression will be given that each has a processor to itself (see Figure 3.2).

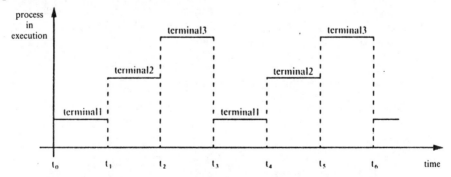

Figure 3.2   Sharing of a single processor among three processes

3.2 PSEUDO-PARALLELISM AND QUASI-PARALLELISM

Sharing of a processor among a number of processes, as just described, is known technically as *pseudo-parallelism*. This is characterized by

- only one process executing at any one instant;
- process switching (meaning changing from executing process p1 to executing p2, as at instants t1, t2, t3, ... in Fig. 3.2) is outside the control of the processes themselves.

Clearly, one would expect a concurrent or a real-time language to provide pseudo-parallel execution, and this is in fact the case with Portal and Ada. Pseudo-parallelism is to be contrasted on the one hand with true parallelism (which requires at least two processors) and on the other with *quasi-parallelism*. The latter is characterized by:

- only one process executing at any one time (as with pseudo-parallelism);
- process switching occurring at the request of the active process (ie the one executing then), as the result of executing a particular instruction.

Quasi-parallel processes are often called coroutines. This type of execution is generally used in simulation, but it is also the execution scheme of Modula-2, which is its original feature. We shall see the importance of this choice in Chapter 7.

3.3 ROLE OF THE KERNEL IN PSEUDO-PARALLELISM

Here, as we have said, process switching is done without reference to the processes themselves. The obvious question is then, what actually does this switching? The answer is a set of procedures called the *kernel*. The term is used on connection with both concurrent (or real-time) languages and operating systems. The kernel is simply an allocator that shares the processor's time among the different processes. We will now explain the main ideas that underlie its working.

3.3.1 Data structures managed by a kernel

The data structures handled by a kernel are essentially *process descriptors*, which are data structures providing all the information relevant to a particular process:

- the variables belonging to the process;
- the priority and status of the process (see following chapters);
- the contents of the process's registers when it is not executing.

30

This is called the *execution context* of the process.

It is usual to hold the process variables on a stack because this enables *re-entrant* procedures to be written – that is, procedures that can be executed by several different processes simultaneously. As an illustration, consider the piece of program given in Figure 3.3. Here each of the procedures p1 and p2 execute the procedure **proc**, and has its own copies of the parameter i and the local variable j in its stack. Figure 3.4 shows the contents of the stacks of processes p1 and p2 immediately after each has executed the instruction j: = i + 5.

```
procedure proc (i: integer);
   var j: integer;
code
   j: = i + 5;
   ...
end proc;

process p1;
   var v1: integer;
code
   v1: = 10;
   proc(v1)
end p1;

process p2;
   var v2: integer;
code
   v2: = 11;
   proc(v2)
end p2;
```

Figure 3.3   Re-entrant procedure

As shown in Figure 3.5 the process stack can be used also to save the processor registers when the process is not executing. Considering the descriptor, if we wish to recover all the information relevant to a process, all we need do is recover that process's stack; this is made possible by including the stack pointer in the descriptor. Therefore, it is sufficient to hold a list of descriptors in the kernel to be able to maintain access to the corresponding processes. Figure 3.5 shows the case of a kernel that manages three processes. Here process p1 is executing and is using the processor registers; processes p2 and p3 are not executing and the processor registers have been saved on top of the respective stacks.

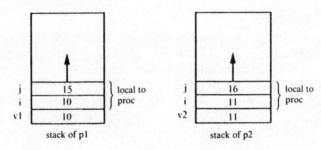

Figure 3.4 Stack contents for processes of Figure 3.3

Thus the list of descriptors is the central data structure of the kernel. We shall discuss this further in the following chapters, where for convenience we shall sometimes use the term 'process list' to mean this list of descriptors.

3.3.2 Process switching

In order to know when to switch processes the kernel uses a peripheral called a *clock* which produces interrupts at regular intervals – typically 50 times per second. At each interrupt the active process (the one then executing) is suspended in favour of another. Figure 3.6a–3.6e [pp 33–5] show the sequence of operations executed by the kernel:

1. The processor registers for the interrupted process are saved on top of its stack (Figure 3.6a). In the PDP-11 the program cunter and the processor

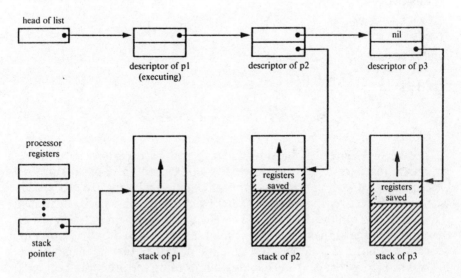

Figure 3.5 List of process descriptors: process p1 is executing

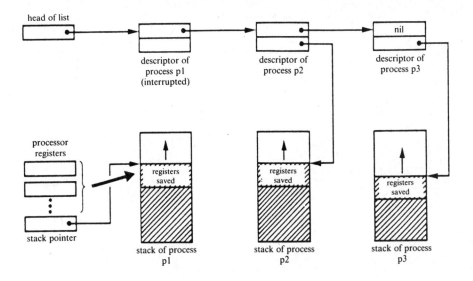

Figure 3.6a   Process p1 interrupted, registers saved on its stack

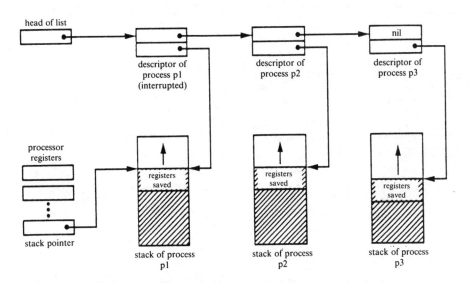

Figure 3.6b   Saving the stack pointer register in the descriptor of process p1

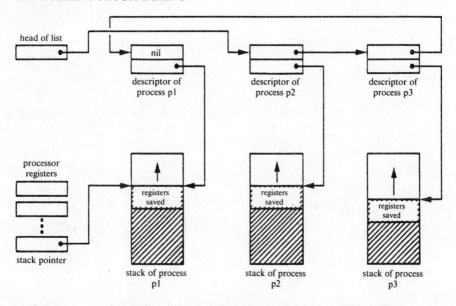

Figure 3.6c Updating the list of descriptors: descriptor for process p1 is moved to the end of the list

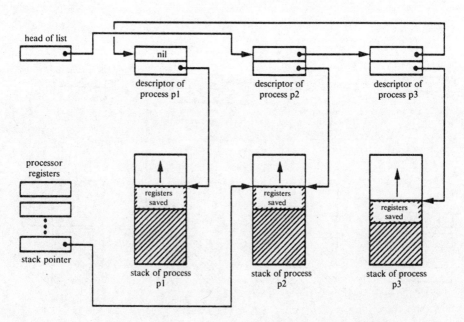

Figure 3.6d Loading the stack pointer register with the value in the descriptor at the head of the list

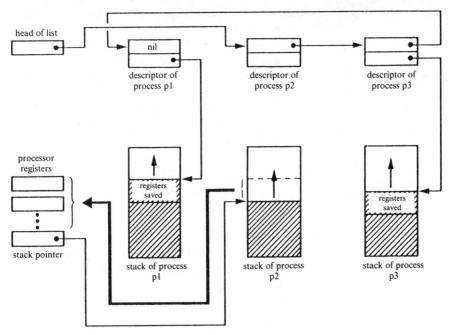

Figure 3.6e   Loading the processor registers with the values saved on the stack of process p2

status register are saved automatically (see 2.3), so the kernel need save only the remaining registers.

2. The stack pointer is saved in the process descriptor (Figure 3.6b).
3. The list of descriptors is updated by moving the descriptor of the interrupted process to the end of the list (Figure 3.6c). Execution of this process will be resumed when its descriptor has worked its way back to the head of the list.
4. The stack pointer is loaded with the value in the descriptor now at the head of the list (Figure 3.6d). This makes it possible to recover the stack of the process to which the kernel has now to allocate the processor.
5. The processor registers are loaded with the values saved on the stack of the process just selected, the program counter last (Figure 3.6e). Execution of the next process now begins.

Here we have mentioned only the interrupts generated by the clock, but the kernel must of course respond to all interrupts, since any interrupt may lead to a process switch. Some further concepts, in particular that of the process state, must be included in a complete kernel. An important point is that all interrupts from peripherals must be disabled while the kernel is executing, for otherwise inconsistencies would certainly result.

An interesting question that arises here is whether it is essential for the kernel to use the clock interrupts to share the processor time among the different processes, or whether it would be adequate for the switching to be done only in response to interrupts from other peripherals. For a time-sharing system such as the one described at the beginning of this chapter, clock switching is essential to avoid the monopolizing of the processor by one user whose commands are compute bound. Clock interrupts would not be used in a purely real-time system in which processes are I/O bound: by the nature of the application, no one process should monopolize the processor. This second case would still be described as pseudo-parallel, since the switching is still done without the process knowing it; the related problems are the same.

3.4   CONCLUSION

The process concept enables us to handle the complexity of a program that has to manage a number of peripheral devices. Such a program typically has a number of processes that are executed in turn, the switching from one to another being made by a kernel in response to interrupts. The process is thus a powerful tool, which must however be used with care. We consider this in the two following chapters.

Chapter 4

MUTUAL EXCLUSION

A concurrent program is made up of a number of processes that are not necessarily independent: it can happen, for example, that several of them need to act on the same variable, or to gain access to the same peripheral. Errors can result in such situations, so some control has to be exerted.

4.1 STATEMENT OF THE PROBLEM

Consider a concurrent program consisting of processes p1 which reads from a disc and p2 which sends characters to a printer. If there is a disc error or any problem with the printer an appropriate message is to be written on the operator console's screen. Thus, for example, process p1 will be led to write DISC ERROR and process p2 to write PRINTER NOT READY when they detect an error. A first naïve program for sharing the console is given in Figure 4.1.

```
module console;
defines write; (* procedure exported by module *)

   procedure write (s: string);
   code
      display each character of string s
   end write;

end console;

process p1;
uses console; (* module imported *)
code
   ...
   console.write ('DISC ERROR');
   ...
end p1;

process p2;
uses console; (* module imported *)
```

code

...

console.write ('PRINTER NOT READY');

...

end p2;

Figure 4.1 Naïve program for sharing the console

This program is faulty because it does not take into account the possibility of processes p1 and p2 needing to write to the console at the same time – that is, of p2 starting to write its message before p1 has finished. This can happen, for example, if process p1, having started to write, loses the processor to p2 which also starts to write. The characters of the two messages then become interwoven and something like DISPRINC ERRTER . . . could appear.

To avoid such mixing up of messages either process must be prevented from calling the procedure console.write while the other is executing it; the console must be accessed in *mutual exclusion*. The same need arises in connection with access to files by an operating system: while one user U1 is modifying a file then no other user U2 must be able to gain access to the same file.

In these examples mutual exclusion has to be applied to access to the console and to the files respectively. These are particular cases of what are called *critical resources*, defined as objects that can be accessed only under mutual exclusion. The term critical section is used to refer to a part of a program in which a process accesses a critical resource. Thus in Figure 4.1 the procedure console.write is a critical section.

To correct the error in Figure 4.1 we constrain access to console.write by means of a module cs ('critical section') which exports procedures start and finish, to be called before and after console.write respectively. This is shown in Figure 4.2.

module cs; (* critical section *)
defines start, finish; (* procedures exported *)

...

end cs;

module console;
defines write; (* procedure exported *)

...

end console;

process p1;
uses cs, console; (* modules imported *)

code

```
   ...
   cs.start;
   console.write ('DISC ERROR');
   cs.finish;
   ...
end p1;

process p2;
uses cs, console; (* modules imported *)
code
   ...
   cs.start;
   console.write ('PRINTER NOT READY');
   cs.finish;
   ...
end p2;
```

Figure 4.2   Inclusion of module cs in program of Figure 4.1

To work correctly the module cs must guarantee that at any instant only one process can be executing between cs.start and cs.finish. In addition the following conditions must hold:

- any process can enter the critical section if no other process is occupying it;
- any process seeking to enter the critical section must be able to do so within a finite time.

That the first should hold is self-evident. The second condition means that access by any process waiting to enter the critical section is not delayed indefinitely by other processes that ask to enter it later.

4.2   MUTUAL EXCLUSION BY BUSY WAITING

Let us now construct the module cs using the means we have at our disposal; Figure 4.3 is our first attempt.

```
1    module cs; (* critical section *)
2    defines start, finish;

3        var busy: boolean;
```

```
4     procedure start;
5     code
6       while busy do end while; (* busy waiting *)
7         busy: = true
8     end start;

9     procedure finish;
10    code
11       busy: = false
12    end finish;

13  code (* initialization *)
14     busy: = false
15  end cs;
```

Figure 4.3   Incorrect implementation of critical section

Unfortunately this solution is not correct. Consider the following situation, with the variable busy initially set to false:

- process p1 (Figure 4.2) calls cs.start. Suppose p1 loses the processor immediately after executing the **while** loop but before the assignment busy: = true, that is, between lines 6 and 7;
- process p2, whose execution is resumed, calls cs.start. The variable busy is false, p2 sets it to true, leaves cs.start and calls console.write (Figure 4.2). It then loses the processor;
- process p1 resumes execution at line 7, leaves cs.start and then also calls console.write.

The conclusion is that a single boolean variable is not sufficient to ensure mutual exclusion. The first solution to overcome the difficulty was proposed by Dekker and is given in [Dijkstra 68]. Figure 4.4 gives a simpler solution due to Peterson [Peterson 81] which, though only valid for two processes, can be generalized to the case of n. Here is the basic idea. If neither p1 nor p2 is trying to enter the critical section then the boolean variable request[3 – no] is false and entry is allowed; but if both are trying simultaneously to enter, the decision is made using the value of the variable turn.

```
1   type noprocess = 1..2;

2   module cs; (* critical section *)
3   defines start, finish;
```

```
 4  var
 5    request: array noprocess of boolean;
 6    turn: noprocess;

 7  procedure start (no: noprocess);
 8  code
 9    request[no]: = true;
10      (* makes request to enter the critical section *)
11    turn: = 3 – no; (* number of the other process *)
12    repeat
13    until (not request[3 – no]) or (turn = no)
14  end start;

15  procedure finish (no: noprocess);
16  code
17    request[no]: = false;
18  end finish;

19  code (* initialization *)
20    request[1]: = false;
21    request[2] = false;
22  end cs;

23  process p1;
24  uses cs, console;
25  code
26    ...
27    cs.start(1);
28    console.write ('DISC ERROR');
29    cs.finish(1);
30    ...
31  end p1;

32  process p2;
33  uses cs, console;
34  code
35    ...
36    cs.start(2);
37    console.write ('PRINTER NOT READY');
38    cs.finish(2);
39    ...
40  end p2;
```

Figure 4.4   Mutual exclusion by busy waiting

41

What happens if process p1 seeks to re-enter the critical section immediately after having left it? It is easily seen that if p2 is waiting at that instant (lines 12, 13 of Figure 4.4) then it gains permission to enter. This guarantees that neither process has to wait indefinitely.

Thus mutual exclusion can be achieved without the need for any new tools. However the satisfaction is purely intellectual. 'Busy waiting' (continual testing of a condition until it is found to hold) is not a realistic method to be used in practice, for the resulting waste of processor time is unacceptable.

4.3   MUTUAL EXCLUSION BY MASKING INTERRUPTS

We saw in Chapter 3 that process switching is triggered by an interrupt generated either by the clock or by any other peripheral. Mutual exclusion can therefore be achieved by masking interrupts: no more interrupts, so no more process switching, and consequently no more chances of violating the exclusion constraints.

The control of access to the console that we have been discussing can then be expressed as follows:

```
process p1;
uses console;
code
    ...
    disable interrupts;
    console.write ('DISC ERROR');
    enable interrupts;
    ...
end p1;
```

with a corresponding code for process p2. This however has two disadvantages:

- it forbids any I/O in interrupt mode in the critical section;
- there is a risk of interrupts being lost if the critical section is long (a device interrupt is lost if the same device generates a second interrupt before the first has been dealt with).

This solution nevertheless can be used if the critical section is short and involves no input or output. We shall return to this in 4.4.

Before going further we should take a brief look at shared memory multiprocessor architectures – that is, architectures in which a number of processors share a common memory. Here nothing is achieved by masking interrupts because the exclusion can be violated by the simple fact of the different processes being executed in parallel. The solution to the problem involves an instruction of the type *test_and_set*, which results in reading a variable and then assigning it a value in an indivisible operation. Such an instruction can be regarded as equivalent to the following function:

```
type state = (free, busy);

function test_and_set (var v: state): state;
code
    test_and_set: = v;
    v: = busy
end test_and_set;
```

Entry into the critical section is then achieved by busy waiting as follows (v corresponds to a location in common memory, and the result of test_and_set is returned to a bit in the status word of the processor that is executing the instruction):

```
repeat
until test_and_set(v) = free;
```

The critical section is left by means of the assignment

```
v: = free;
```

The memory access mechanism will prevent two processors from executing the test_and_set instruction simultaneously, so mutual exclusion is guaranteed and the first to execute the instruction gains access. Busy waiting is not too wasteful here provided that the critical section is short.

Treating the problem of mutual exclusion in multiprocessor systems that do not have a common memory would take us outside the scope of this book. The interested reader should consult for example [Raynal 84].

4.4 MUTUAL EXCLUSION USING LOCKS

We now introduce the most primitive tool which enables mutual exclusion to be achieved without either busy waiting or interrupt masking. This tool is called a *lock*, which is a variable of the following type:

```
type lock_type = record
                    state: (open, closed);
                    waiting: list of processes
                end record;
```

A lock has two possible states, open or closed (initially it is open). It also contains a list of processes, namely the processes waiting at the closed lock. A process never has access to the fields of a lock; it can act on a lock only by means of the two procedures lock and unlock that are defined as follows:

```
procedure lock (var v: lock_type);
code
  if v.state = open then v.state: = closed
  else block process in list 'v.waiting'
  end if
end lock;

procedure unlock (var v: lock_type);
code
  if list 'v.waiting' not empty then awaken a process of list 'v.waiting'
  else v.state: = open
  end if
end unlock;
```

Of course these procedures are critical sections too – the critical resource here being the lock. However, as they are very short and involve neither input nor output, they can be implemented using the techniques of 4.3.

We can now write the code for accessing the console as follows:

```
var v: lock_type;

process p1;
uses console;
code
  . . .
  lock(v);
  console.write('DISC ERROR');
  unlock(v);
  . . .
end p1;
```

with a corresponding code for process p2.

The procedures lock and unlock are called mutual exclusion primitives, a term that indicates that they are indivisible operations: a process that starts to execute either will not lose the processor before completing the execution.

A more complete description of these primitives is given in Figure 4.5, where they are incorporated into a kernel. This makes clearer the meaning of blocking and awakening a process. The list ready_processes (line 9) contains all the processes that are not blocked – that is, all those that are not waiting at a closed lock. Only these processes are candidates for getting the processor (lines 19, 20). Thus blocking a process consists simply in removing it from the 'ready' list (lines 15, 16), so it cannot get the processor. Awakening a process consists in returning it to the 'ready' list (lines 28, 29). The waiting list (line 6) contains those processes that are temporarily blocked; it is managed using a FIFO policy, so no process will have to wait indefinitely at a lock.

```
 1   module kernel; (* executed with interrupts disabled *)
 2   defines lock_type, lock, unlock;

 3   type
 4     lock_type = record
 5                     state: (open, closed);
 6                     waiting: list of processes
 7                 end record;

 8   var
 9     ready_processes: list of processes;
10         (* processes that can be given the processor *)

11   procedure lock (var v: lock_type);
12   code
13     if v.state = open then v.state: = closed
14     else
15       remove process from list 'ready_processes'
16       and queue it on tail of the list
17       'v.waiting';
18           (* execution of this process stops *)
19       take the process at the head of the list
20       'ready_processes' and resume its execution
21           (* a new process is executed *)
22     end if
23   end lock;

24   procedure unlock (var v: lock_type);
25   code
26     if list 'v.waiting' not empty
27     then
28       take process at head of list 'v. waiting'
29       and queue it on tail of the list 'ready_processes'
30           (* this process will be executed later *)
```

```
31          (* a better choice might be to put this process
32            at the head of the 'ready_processes' list,
33            so that it is executed immediately *)
34      else
35          v.state: = open
36      end if
37    end unlock;

38  code (* initialization *)
39    initialize list 'ready_processes'
40  end kernel;
```

Figure 4.5   A kernel implementing locks

This kernel is not really complete, because it includes no handling of interrupts. We will take this up in Chapter 7 where we describe the language Modula-2, a language in which kernels can be written.

4.5   MUTUAL EXCLUSION USING SEMAPHORES

We have just seen how a critical section can be implemented using locks. A lock, however, is a relatively primitive tool, in the sense that it is not suited for the solution of more complicated problems. Consider, for example, the problem of allocating m printers to n processes, where $n > m$. Any process may request a printer, use it, and then release it. If no printer is free when the request is issued then the process must wait, and will be re-activated when some other process releases a printer. If there is only one printer we are back to the critical section problem, but let us consider the general case. Use of locks is awkward here, whereas the problem is easily solved with the aid of the semaphore, a tool proposed by Dijkstra in 1968 [Dijkstra 68].

A *semaphore* is a variable of the following type:

```
Type semaphore = record
                    n: integer;
                    waiting: list of processes
                 end record
```

This is a generalization of the lock. In the latter the field state can take only two values, but here it is replaced by a field n of integer type. As for a lock, no process can access the fields of a semaphore directly, and handling is possible only by means of primitives called P and V by Dijkstra. These are defined as follows:

46

```
procedure P (var s: semaphore);
code
    s.n: = s.n – 1;
    if s.n < 0 then block the calling process at tail of list 's.waiting'
    end if
end P;

procedure V (var s: semaphore);
code
    s.n: = s.n + 1;
    if s.n ≤ 0 then awaken the process at head of list 's.waiting'
    end if
end V;
```

As with lock and unlock, the procedures P and V constitute a critical section that can be implemented using the methods described in §4.3. The careful reader will have noticed that if s.n ≤ 0, the absolute value |s.n| is the number of blocked processes in the list s.waiting. This explains why, in V, after s.n has been incremented a process is released only if s.n ≤ 0: if s.n > 0 (meaning that s.n ⩾ 0 before the incrementation), no process is in the waiting list.

How the field n of a semaphore has to be initialized is not self-evident, but depends on the type of problem. For a critical section it must be initialized to 1 (which is indicated using the keyword **init** in the declaration).

```
var mutex: semaphore init 1;

process pi; (* i = 1, 2, ...: code for processes p1, p2, ... *)
code
    ...
    P (mutex);
    (* critical section *)
    V(mutex);
    ...
end pi;
```

The identifier mutex is an abbreviation of *mutual exclusion*. Since mutex.n has been initialized to 1, the first call of P(mutex) does not block the process, but the second one does. This is the key to the achieving of mutual exclusion using semaphores.

We can demonstrate the superiority of semaphores over locks by returning to the problem of allocating printers. Figure 4.6 gives the semaphore solution, in which the two semaphores mutex and free_printers play distinct roles. The semaphore mutex implements the critical sections of lines 20–24 and line 30, in which the critical resource is the array allocated indicating for each printer whether or not it is being used. The semaphore free_printers enables a process in the procedure allocate to be blocked if no printer is available. This second semaphore is of course initialized to m, the number of printers provided, so that the first m calls of P(free_printers) do not result in any blocking. Subsequent calls will block processes unless in the meantime calls to V(free_printers) have been made.

```
1    module printer;
2    defines allocate, release;

3      const
4         m = ...; (* number of printers *)

5      var
6         allocated: array 1 .. m of boolean;
7            (* gives the state of each printer *)
8         i: integer; (* see initialization code *)

9         mutex: semaphore init 1;
10            (* semaphore for mutual exclusion *)
11        free_printers: semaphore init m;
12            (* semaphore for waiting for a printer *)

13     procedure allocate (var printer_no: integer);
14     code
15        P(free_printers);

16        (* when a process reaches this line there is at
17           least one printer available; we now have
18           to determine which one *)
19        P(mutex);
20        printer_no: = 1;
21        while allocated[printer_no] do
22           printer_no: = printer_no + 1;
23        end while;
24        allocated[printer_no]: = true;
25        V(mutex)
26     end allocate;

27     procedure release (var printer_no: integer);
28     code
```

```
29    P(mutex);
30    allocated[printer_no]: = false;
31    V(mutex);
32    (* P(mutex) and V(mutex) can be
33       omitted here *)
34    V(free_printers);
35  end release;

36  code (* initialization *)
37     for i: = 1 to m do allocated[i]: = false end for
38  end printer;

39  process pi; (* i = 1, 2, ...: code for processes p1, p2, ... *)
40  uses printer;
41     var no: integer;
42  code
43     ...
44     printer.allocate(no);
45     write to printer(no);
46     printer.release(no);
47     ...
48  end pi;
```

Figure 4.6   Allocation of printers using semaphores

An error easily made with semaphores is to include a call to the primitive P inside a critical section. This would be the case if the order of the calls to P(mutex) and P(free_printers), in lines 15 and 19 respectively, were inverted. If this were done, a process p1 blocked by the call to P(free_printers) would never be awakened: any process p2 wishing to release a printer would be blocked by the call to P(mutex) of line 29, because p1 is still occupying the critical section protected by the semaphore mutex. This situation is called *deadlock*: each process is blocking the other, p1 blocking p2 through the semaphore mutex, p2 blocking p1 through free_printers.

A final point to be noted here is that while the order in which the primitives P are executed is important, as we have just seen, the same is not true for V. The solution given in Figure 4.6 remains correct if the calls to V(mutex) and V(free_printers), in lines 31 and 34 respectively, are inverted.

4.6   THE READERS/WRITERS PROBLEM

There are a number of classical problems in concurrent programming, designed for the specific purpose of evaluating a synchronization primitive (mutual exclusion being a particular case of synchronization). The printer allocation problem enabled us to demonstrate the superiority of semaphores over locks. We will now study another classical problem, the readers and writers problem [Courtois 71]. This is a variant on the mutual exclusion problem, with which we can evaluate the usefulness of semaphores for solving more complex problems.

We will consider here two kinds of processes – readers and writers. The readers wish to read certain data, say a file, and the writers wish to modify them. We need to ensure mutual exclusion among the writers on the one hand and between readers and writers on the other. There must be no simultaneous writing by two processes because this would produce meaningless data. In the same way writing during reading would result in meaningless data being read. However when no writing is being done two or more readers may access the same data simultaneously.

This does not quite define the problem completely. Consider the situation in which a reader process r1 is reading when a writer w1 arrives, shortly followed by a second reader r2. If we wish the readers to have priority over the writers we must allow r2 to read immediately. If the writers are to have priority then process r2 must wait until w1 has completed its writing. There are three cases to distinguish:

- priority to the readers
- priority to the writers
- same priority to both, with access given in order of arrival.

Suppose that while some process is writing several processes arrive in the order below:

r1, r2, w1, r3, w2.

When the current process is completed, access to the data can be allowed in one of the following orders, according to the priority rule chosen:

- priority to readers: r1, r2, r3; then w1; then w2;
- priority to writers: w1; then w2; then r1, r2, r3;
- equal priorities: r1, r2; then w1; then r3; then w2.

To formalize this we use a notation given in [Robert 77]. Consider a procedure p and let us introduce:

- #act(p), the number of processes currently executing procedure p;
- #wait(p), the number of processes waiting to execute procedure p.

In our problem p can be either read or write, and the simplest statement of the readers/writers problem is:

- reading is allowed if #act(write) = 0;
- writing is allowed if #act(write) = 0 and #act(read) = 0.

Readers priority is expressed by:

- reading is allowed if #act(write) = 0;
- writing is allowed if
  #act(write) = 0 and #act(read) = 0 and #wait(read) = 0.

Correspondingly, writers priority is expressed by:

- reading is allowed if #act(write) = 0 and #wait(write) = 0;
- writing is allowed if #act(write) = 0 and #act(read) = 0.

The notation introduced takes no account of the order of arrival of the processes and therefore does not allow us to express the case of equal priorities.

We will now show how semaphors can be used to solve the readers/ writers problem when the priorities are equal (the case of readers' priority is no more complicated, but that of writers' priority is much more difficult).

A first outline of the solution for equal priorities is as follows:

```
var rw: semaphore init 1;

process reader;
code
  P(rw);
  V(rw);
  READ;
end reader;

process writer;
code
  P(rw);
  WRITE;
  V(rw);
end writer;
```

The semaphore rw is used by both readers and writers. Since the list of processes waiting at a semaphore is handled as a FIFO queue, the processes here are given access to the data in the order in which they arrive – that is readers and writers have same priority. However, the above program implements only the conditions:

51

- reading allowed if #act(write) = 0;
- writing allowed if #act(write) = 0.

So we must do something to prevent writing during reading. For this purpose we add a second semaphore w, at which the writers wait while a process is reading. The program is given in Figure 4.7. Notice here the conditional executions of P(w) before reading (line 9) and of V(w) after reading (line 13): the first reader, when starting to read, prevents the writers from gaining access to the data and the last to finish reading allows the access again.

```
1   var
2       nbr_readers: integer; (* initialized to 0 *)
3       rw: semaphore init 1;
4       w: semaphore init 1;

5   process reader;
6   code
7       P(rw);
8       nbr_readers: = nbr_readers + 1;
9       if nbr_readers = 1 then P(w) end if;
10      V(rw);
11      READ;
12      nbr_readers: = nbr_readers – 1;
13      if nbr_readers = 0 then V(w) end if
14  end reader;

15  process writer;
16  code
17      P(rw);
18      P(w);
19      WRITE;
20      V(w);
21      V(rw);
22  end writer;
```

Figure 4.7 Readers/writers problem: sketch of solution with equal priorities

This solution is still not completely correct: the variable nbr_readers is a critical resource, access to which must be protected by a semaphore mutex. This is incorporated into the final version given in Figure 4.8. Here the form is that of a module that exports the procedures start_read, finish_read, start_write and finish_write.

```
module readers_writers;
defines start_read, finish_read, start_write, finish_write;
var
    nbr_readers: integer;
    rw: semaphore init 1;
    w: semaphore init 1;
    mutex: semaphore init 1;

procedure start_read;
code
    P(rw);
    P(mutex);
    nbr_readers: = nbr_readers + 1;
    if nbr_readers = 1 then P(w) end if;
    V(mutex);
    V(rw);
end start_read;

procedure finish_read;
code
    P(mutex);
    nbr_readers: = nbr_readers - 1;
    if nbr_readers = 0 then V(w) end if;
    V(mutex)
end finish_read;

procedure start_write;
code
    P(rw);
    P(w);
end start_write;

procedure finish_write;
code
    V(w);
    V(rw);
end finish_write;

code (* initialization *)
    nbr_readers: = 0;
end readers_writers;
```

Figure 4.8 Readers/writers problem, with equal priorities: solution using semaphores

4.7 EXERCISES

4.7.1 Figure 4.4 gives a solution to the mutual exclusion problem, using busy waiting. Is the solution still correct if the order of lines 9 and 11 is inverted?

4.7.2 Generalize the solution of Figure 4.4 to the case of n processes.

4.7.3 Give a solution to the printer-allocation problem (§4.5) using locks.

4.7.4 Construct a semaphore solution of the printer-allocation problem for the case in which a process can request either one or two printers. A request for two will be granted only if two are free, a single free printer being left available to satisfy a later request for one printer. When printers are released give priority to processes requesting two.

4.7.5 In the readers/writers solution of Figure 4.8, what happens if the calls to P(rw) in start_write and V(rw) in finish_write are removed?

4.7.6 Give a semaphore solution to the readers/writers problem with priority to the readers.

4.7.7 Give a corresponding solution with priority to the writers.

Chapter 5

COOPERATION BETWEEN PROCESSES

In Chapter 4 we considered the case of processes competing for access to a critical resource. But competition is not the only type of relation between processes; they may also need to cooperate. In this chapter we will discuss the different ways in which cooperation can be expressed.

5.1 STATEMENT OF THE PROBLEM

The need for cooperation between different processes arises most commonly when data have to be transferred from one to another. Consider the simplest possible case: a process **keyboard** reads a character typed on the keyboard of a terminal and transmits it to a process **screen** that displays the character on the screen at the same terminal (ie the second process 'echoes' the character read).

```
            var c: char;

            process keyboard;
               var char_read: char;
            code
               read a character from the keyboard into the variable
               char_read;
```

statement S1 → | c: = char_read |

```
            end keyboard;

            process screen:
               var char_to_write: char;
            code
```

statement S2 → | char_to_write: = c; |

```
               write character char_to_write on the screen
            end screen;
```

55

We will suppose for simplicity that only one character is read from the keyboard – that is, the processes don't loop. Clearly, process screen cannot execute statement S2 until keyboard has completed statement S1 and must therefore be stopped if it tries to execute statement S2 before a character has become available. This is called synchronizing the two processes, which means that an order must be imposed on their execution. Mutual exclusion as studied in Chapter 4 is a particular case of synchronization: a process may not enter a critical section before the preceding occupying process has left it.

5.2   SYNCHRONIZATION USING EVENTS

The *event* is the simplest tool for achieving synchronization. Events are variables whose type is defined as follows:

```
type event = record
                occurred: boolean;
                waiting: list of processes;
             end record;
```

An event either has occurred or has not occurred (initially it has not occurred). The associated waiting list consists of all the processes that are waiting for the event to occur. So far the analogy between events and locks is striking. The operations defined for each are however different, being specifically adapted to their particular aims: the lock to mutual exclusion and the event to synchronization.

An event can be manipulated by means of the procedures *wait*, *trigger* and *reset*, defined as follows:

```
procedure wait (var e: event);
code
  if not e.occurred then
     block the process in the list 'e.waiting'
  end if
end wait;

procedure trigger (var e: event);
code
   e.occurred: = true;
   awaken all processes waiting in the list 'e.waiting'
end trigger;

procedure reset (var e: event);
```

```
code
    e.occurred: = false
end reset;
```

Using events and these procedures we can now write the keyboard and screen processes of §5.1 as follows:

```
var
    c: char;
    e: event; (* initially not occurred *)

process keyboard;
    var char_read: char;
code
    read a character from the keyboard into the variable char_read;
    c: = char_read;
    trigger(e);
end keyboard;

process screen;
    var char_to_write: char;
code
    wait(e);
    char_to_write: = c;
    write the character char_to_write on the screen;
end screen;
```

Process screen is blocked if and only if it executes wait(e) before process keyboard has executed trigger(e); thus the synchronization is expressed correctly.

The event is a primitive tool, not well adapted to the solution of more complicated problems (see the exercises at the end of this chapter). Further, mutual exclusion cannot be realized with the operations described above. This is sometimes rectified by introducing procedure trigger in a slightly different form:

```
procedure test_and_trigger (var e: event; var occurred: boolean);
code
    occurred: = e.occurred;
    e.occurred: = true;
    awaken all processes waiting in list 'e.waiting'
end test_and_trigger;
```

This procedure saves the value of an event before triggering it. The semantics is similar to that of test_and_set (§4.3), and in the same way enables the implementation of mutual exclusion by busy waiting.

5.3   SYNCHRONIZATION USING SEMAPHORES

Semaphores were introduced in §4.5. We may recall here that a semaphore consists of an integer variable together with a list of waiting processes. It is handled by two procedures – P which decrements the integer variable and blocks the process if the variable becomes negative, and V which increments the variable and awakens a waiting process if any. In §4.5 the semaphore was presented as a generalization of the lock. It can also be considered as a generalization of the event.

The keyboard/screen problem that we have been discussing is solved in terms of semaphores (initialized to 0) as follows:

```
var
    c: char;
    s: semaphore init 0;

process keyboard;
    var char_read: char;
code
    read a character from the keyboard into the variable char_read;
    c: = char_read;
    V(s);
end keyboard;

process screen;
    var char_to_write: char;
code
    P(s);
    char_to_write: = c;
    write the character char_to_write on the screen;
end screen;
```

Process screen is blocked if and only if it executes P(s) before process keyboard has executed V(s), and if blocked it is awakened when keyboard executes V(s). Thus correct synchronization is achieved. The above semaphores are said to be private to the process screen: only this process executes the procedure P(s) and can be blocked in the waiting list of s.

5.4 SYNCHRONIZATION USING MONITORS

In the same way as the semaphore was shown to be a better tool than both the lock and the event, so will the monitor appear to have advantages over the semaphore. However, instead of defining a data structure and primitives that act on it, we will now define the monitor as a syntactic unit with properties that ensure mutual exclusion, and in which we will express the desired synchronization. The concept is due to Hoare [Hoare 74]; we describe it here using the syntax of the Portal language.

A monitor is a syntactic unit similar to a module. It enables variables, and procedures that act on those variables, to be grouped together. In addition, the monitor imposes mutual exclusion on the procedures declared inside it. In other words, if a process p1 is executing a procedure p of a monitor m, then a process p2 calling p or any other procedure of m will be temporarily blocked. Process p2's call will be allowed when p1 either leaves m or, as we shall see, executes the procedure wait.

Synchronization within a monitor is expressed using *signals* together with the procedures *wait* and *send* (see Figure 5.1). If s is a signal, execution of s.wait blocks a process unconditionally; the blocked process is said to be waiting for the signal s. It is awakened by the execution of s.send. Several processes can be waiting for the same signal[1], the execution of s.send will awaken only one process, the one at the head of the signal's queue. The procedure wait has an essential property: when a process is blocked as a result of executing s.wait the mutual exclusion on the monitor is released. This is a crucial point and solves the main problem encountered when using semaphores. Consider the following example:

```
1  var
2     mutex: semaphore init 1;
3     s: semaphore init 0;

4  process p1;
5  code
6     ...
7     P(mutex);
8     if c1 then P(s) end if;
9     (* other instructions *)
10    V(mutex);
11    ...
12 end p1;
```

[1] In Portal the boolean function s.awaited() enables us to find if the signal s is expected; the function returns the value true if the signal's queue contains at least one process.

```
13  process p2;
14  code
15    ...
16    P(mutex);
17    if c2 then V(s) end if;
18    V(mutex);
19    ...
20  end p2;
```

If the execution of P(s) blocks p1 (line 8) there is a deadlock; process p1 can never be awakened by p2 since p2 is inside the critical section protected by the semaphore mutex. This situation occurs naturally in the expression of many synchronization problems (see exercise 4.7.4). The potential deadlock can be avoided by expressing p1 differently:

```
1   process p1;
2   code
3     ...
4     P(mutex);
5     if c1 then
6       V(mutex); (* leave the critical section *)
7       P(s); (* the process is possibly blocked *)
8       P(mutex); (* return to the critical section *)
9     end if;
10    (* other statements *)
11    V(mutex);
12    ...
13  end p1;
```

In line 6 process p1 takes the precaution of leaving the critical section. However, there is no guarantee that the condition c1 is still true when p1 executes P(s) (line 7), since some other process could have invalidated c1 between p1's execution of V(mutex) and P(s) – that is between lines 6 and 7. Process p1 should execute V(mutex) and P(s) without losing the processor. This is achieved by the semantics of monitors, the mutual exclusion being released by execution of the primitive wait.

Figure 5.1 gives the monitor solution for the keyboard/screen problem. Here m is a monitor that exports procedures put_char (called by process keyboard) and get_char (called by process screen).

```
1   monitor m;
2   defines put_char, get_char;
```

```
3    var
4      c: char;
5      char_available: boolean;

6    signal s:
7      (* carries the condition 'char_available = true' *)

8      procedure get_char (var ch: char);
9      code
10       if not char_available then s.wait end if;
11       ch: = c;
12     end get_char;

13     procedure put_char (ch: char);
14     code
15       c: = ch;
16       car_available: = true;
17       s.send (* awakens the process waiting for s *)
18
19     end put_char;

20   code (* initialization *)
21       char_available: = false;
22   end m;

23   process keyboard;
24   uses m;
25     var char_read: char;
26   code
27     read a character from the keyboard into the variable char_read;
28     m.put_char (char_read);
29   end keyboard;

31   process screen;
31   uses m;
32     var char_to_write: char;
33   code
34     m.get_char (char_to_write);
35     write the character char_to_write on the screen
36   end screen;
```

Figure 5.1 Synchronization of processes keyboard and screen using a monitor

The synchronization is expressed in the monitor m using the variable char_available and the signal s, which carries the condition char_available = true. The process screen waits for the signal s if and only if this variable has the value false (line 10). The monitor enforces mutual exclusion on get_char and put_char, thus ensuring that char_available cannot be tested by screen (line 10) while keyboard is modifying it (line 16). If process screen is blocked waiting for s (line 10), the monitor's mutual exclusion is released, allowing process keyboard to wake up screen by executing s.send (line 17). It is important to note that process keyboard becomes temporarily suspended after executing s.send. Process screen then becomes the active process in the monitor. This guarantees that the condition char_available = true, carried by signal s, still holds when process screen resumes execution. Process keyboard becomes the active process again when screen leaves the monitor.

With the semantics of send thus established we can now examine lines 10 and 11 of Figure 5.1 more rigorously:

```
10   if not char_available then s.wait end if;
11   ch: = c;
```

We can guarantee that char_available has the value true when line 11 is executed: either it was true already at line 10 or the process is blocked and awakened by s, which carries the condition char_available = true. Note finally that if no process is waiting for s, the execution of s.send has no effect; there is no memorization of sending a signal.

This example is really too simple to show the superiority of monitors over semaphores. Other examples in this book, in particular that of readers and writers (§4.6) which we will come back to in Chapter 6, will prove more convincing.

5.5   THE PRODUCER/CONSUMER PROBLEM

The producer/consumer problem is a generalization of the keyboard/screen problem first introduced in §5.1. In the latter process keyboard plays the role of producer and process screen that of consumer, the number of characters transmitted being limited to one. In the general case the information transmitted consists of an arbitrary number of messages of any type (but of fixed length). The communication takes place within the following framework:

- the producer generates messages and deposits them in a memory area shared by the two processes; we assume that this memory area has capacity for n messages, where $n > 0$;
- the consumer takes messages from this memory area;
- the messages in the shared area are handled using a FIFO policy.

The activities of the two processes, producer and consumer respectively, are shown in Figure 5.2. The messages are handled by the module buffer (a buffer being a shared memory area). Figure 5.3 shows how an array is used to implement the queue. The variable inpt gives the location in which the next message is to be stored and outpt the location from which the next message is to be removed. These variables are incremented modulo n, the size of the array (and the capacity of the buffer), so that the next location after n is location 1.

```
module buffer;
defines put, get;
  . . .
end buffer;

process producer;
uses buffer;
code
  loop
    produce a message;
    buffer.put (message);
  end loop
end producer;

process consumer;
uses buffer;
code
  loop
    buffer.get (message);
    use the message;
  end loop
end consumer;
```

Figure 5.2   Activities of the producer and consumer processes

The synchronization problem to be solved here is the following:

- if the buffer is full when the producer wishes to deposit a message then the producer must be blocked;
- if the buffer is empty when the consumer wishes to take a message then the consumer must be blocked;
- a blocked producer must be awakened as soon as the consumer removes a message, the buffer then being no longer full;
- a blocked consumer must be awakened as soon as the producer deposits a message, the buffer then being no longer empty.

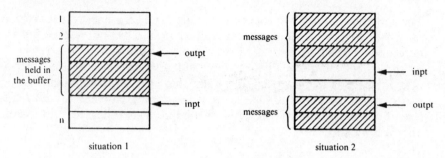

Figure 5.3   Management of a circular buffer

Before expressing this synchronization let us put the producer/consumer problem in its context. As with the readers/writers problem it provides a means for evaluating synchronization mechanisms. Moreover, it corresponds to a situation that arises in every concurrent program. The keyboard/screen problem is an example. Another, which we now discuss briefly, is that of a personal computer emulating a terminal connected to a host mainframe, as in Figure 5.4. Here a character typed on the keyboard goes to the PC (arrow 1) which transmits it to the host (arrow 2); the latter echoes it back to the PC (arrow 3) which causes it to be displayed on the screen (arrow 4). Figure 5.5 shows how the PC program can be expressed using four processes. Here we have the producer/consumer problem twice: once between processes keyboard and sender (the process sending the characters on the line for transmission to the host) and once between processes receiver (which receives characters from the host) and screen.

We can use this example to answer an important question: what is the advantage of putting a buffer that can hold more than one message between a producer and a consumer? The answer is that the greater the buffer's capacity, the better it is able to absorb temporary differences between the rates of production and consumption. Thus if process screen can display characters at a maximum rate of 500 per second, and over some short interval process receiver receives characters at over 500 per second, the extra characters are stored in the buffer and will not be lost. Of course, if reception continues at this high rate for long enough, any buffer whatever its capacity will become full. When this happens, process receiver is blocked and characters put on the line by the host will be lost. Blocking the producer when the buffer is full does not necessarily have disastrous consequences. Consider, for example, a buffer for messages that contain instructions to transfer data between a disc and the main memory: if the buffer is full no further instructions can be taken into account, but there is no loss of information. It still remains that the larger the buffer capacity, the better any temporary differences in rates can be absorbed and the greater the mutual independence of the processes. This leads to better use of the processor by reducing its probability of being idle.

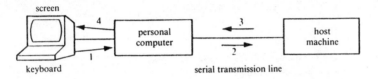

Figure 5.4   Use of a personal computer as a terminal to a host machine

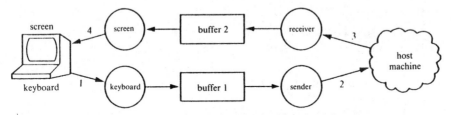

Figure 5.5   Emulation of the terminal of Figure 5.4 by four processes (shown as circles)

We shall now solve the producer/consumer problem, using monitors and semaphores respectively. The monitor solution requires two signals, the semaphore solution two semaphores. Use of events yields a less elegant solution, in which 2n events are needed if the buffer capacity is n messages. This is left to the reader as an exercise (see 5.8.2).

5.5.1   Monitor solution

Consider the program of Figure 5.6. In this solution two signals are used. Although a single one is enough in the case of one producer and one consumer, the solution with two signals is more natural. These signals are:

- non_full, which carries the condition nbr_mess < n, where nbr_mess is the number of messages in the buffer and n the buffer's capacity;
- non_empty, which carries the condition nbr_mess > 0.

If the producer wishes to put a message when the buffer is full it is blocked waiting for the signal non_full (line 16). After putting a message it sends the signal non_empty (line 21), because then the condition nbr_mess > 0 is true. Similarly, if the consumer wishes to remove a message when the buffer is empty it waits for the signal non_empty (line 26), and after removing a message sends the signal non_full, because then nbr_mess < n is true.

```
1   monitor buffer;
2   defines put, get;

3       const
```

```
4      n = 100; (* capacity of buffer *)

5    var
6      buff: array 1 .. n of message; (* buffer *)
7      nbr_mess: integer;
8        (* number of messages in the buffer *)
9      inpt, outpt: 1 .. n; (* see Figure 5.3 *)

10   signal
11     non_full; (* carries condition nbr_mess < n *)
12     non_empty; (* carries condition nbr_mess > 0 *)

13   procedure put (m: message);
14   code
15     if nbr_mess = n then (* buffer full *)
16        non full.wait
17     end if;
18     buff[inpt]: = m; (* puts the message *)
19     inpt: = inpt rem n + 1; (* rem: remainder after the division *)
20     nbr_mess: = nbr_mess + 1;
21     non_empty.send (* since now nbr_mess > 0 *)
22   end put;

23   procedure get (var m: message);
24   code
25     if nbr_mess = then (* buffer empty *)
26        non_empty.wait
27     end if
28     m: = buff[outpt]; (* takes the message *)
29     outpt = outpt rem n + 1;
30     nbr_mess: = nbr_mess - 1;
31     non_full.send (* since now nbr_mess < n *)
32   end get;

33 code (* initialization *)
34   nbr_mess: = 0;
35   inpt: = 1; outpt: = 1;
36 end buffer;
```

Figure 5.6 Monitor solution to the producer/consumer problem

5.5.2 Semaphore solution

The solution is given in Figure 5.7. Two semaphores are needed:

- nbr_mess, which counts the number of messages in the buffer. This semaphore is therefore initialized to 0;
- nbr_free, which counts the number of unoccupied locations in the buffer; it is initialized to n, the buffer capacity.

Quite naturally the producer executes P(nbr_free) before attempting to deposit a message (line 12). This call will block the producer if the number of free locations is zero, meaning that the buffer is full. After putting a message the producer executes V(nbr_mess) (line 15) since the buffer then contains one more message. Similarly the consumer executes P(nbr_mess) before removing a message (line 19) and therefore is blocked if the buffer is empty. Finally it calls V(nbr_free) after removing a message since there is then one more free location in the buffer.

```
1   buffer;
2   defines put, get;

3     const
4       n = 100; (* capacity of buffer *)

5     var
6       buff: array 1 .. n of message; (* buffer *)
7       inpt, outpt: 1 .. n; (* see Figure 5.3 *)

8       nbr_mess: semaphore init 0;
9       nbr_free: semaphore init n;

10    procedure put (m: message);
11    code
12      P(nbr_free);
13      buff[inpt]: = m; (* puts the message *)
14      inpt: = inpt rem n + 1;
15      V(nbr_mess);
16    end put;

17    procedure get (var m: message);
18    code
19      P(nbr_mess);
20      m: = buff[outpt]; (* takes the message *)
```

```
21      outpt: = outpt rem n + 1;
22      V(nbr_free)
23   end get;

24   code (* initialization *)
25     inpt: = 1; outpt: = 1;
26   end buffer;
```

Figure 5.7   Semaphore solution to the producer/consumer problem

Comparing the monitor and semaphore solutions we see that the latter does not need the variable nbr_mess giving the number of messages in the buffer. This is not surprising, because the semaphore contains an implicit counter. Further, the absence of any mutual exclusion constraint on the variables inpt and outpt, and on the array buff, is not an oversight. With only one producer and one consumer inpt and outpt are each manipulated by only a single process, and the synchronization guarantees that producer and consumer can never be given simultaneous access to the same element of buff.

5.6   THE MAILBOX: SYNCHRONIZATION BY DATA

The solutions to the producer/consumer problem given above involve:

- on the one hand, the introduction of an array of messages, common to the two processes, through which the processes communicate;
- on the other, correct synchronization of the two activities of the processes.

If the synchronization required between two processes is only of the producer/consumer kind, we can imagine a mechanism that provides both synchronization and communication. This tool is the *mailbox*, a variable upon which the two operations *mail* and *receive* are defined as follows:

- mail(b, mess) puts message mess in the mailbox b;
- receive(b, mess) removes message mess from the mailbox b. In the mailbox the messages are handled using a FIFO policy.

A process that executes receive(b, mess) when b is empty is blocked, and awakened by the first process that executes mail(b, mess). This is equivalent to saying that a consumer process is blocked until a data item becomes available in the mailbox, hence the term synchronization by data used to describe this mechanism.

A mailbox can of course be implemented using an array of fixed size, just like the message buffer of figure 5.3. A process that executes mail when the mailbox is full will then be blocked. This, however, is only a consequence of the implementation. It is not of the same nature as blocking a process executing receive when the mailbox is empty.

Figure 5.8 gives the mailbox solution for the producer/consumer problem.

```
var b: mailbox of message;
      (* message = type of the values contained in the mailbox b *)

process producer;
  var mess: message;
code
  loop
    produce message 'mess';
    mail (b, mess);
  end loop
end producer;

process consumer;
  var mess: message;
code
  loop
    receive (b, mess);
    use message 'mess';
  end loop
end consumer;
```

Figure 5.8   Mailbox solution to the producer/consumer problem

5.7   THE RENDEZVOUS: STRONG SYNCHRONIZATION BY DATA

The mailbox is not the only type of synchronization by data that can be considered. In 1978 C A R Hoare [Hoare 78] suggested another one which was later adopted, although in a rather different syntactic form, by the designers of the Ada language. This type of synchronization uses the two following commands:

- the output command, written P!e, where P is the name of a process and e an expression;
- the input command, written P?v, where P is again a process name and v a variable.

The process that executes P!e is asking for the expression e to be sent to a process P; the process executing P?v is asking to receive in the variable v a value sent by process P. The input command, of course, blocks the requesting process until it has received the information. In the same way the output command blocks the sending process until the destination process has executed the corresponding input command. This is illustrated in the following example:

```
1   process producer;
2     var mess: message;
3   code
4     loop
5       produce the message 'mess';
6       consumer!mess (* output *)
7     end loop
8   end producer;

9   process consumer;
10    var mess: message;
11  code
12    loop
13      producer? mess; (* input *)
14      use the message 'mess'
15    end loop
16  end consumer;
```

The producer is blocked if it executes the output command of line 6 before the consumer has executed the input command of line 13. Correspondingly, the consumer is blocked if it executes line 13 before the producer has executed line 6. The synchronization can therefore be described as strong: the producer executes the output command (line 6) *exactly* when the consumer executes the corresponding input command (line 13). This is expressed by saying that there is a *rendezvous* between the two processes, and the communication (the transfer of the message) takes place at the moment of the rendezvous.

The solution just given is not equivalent to any of the three given previously, using monitors, semaphores and mailboxes respectively. Here there is no buffer to allow for temporary differences in input and output rates. For an equivalent rendezvous solution a third process must be added to provide a buffer:

- the process buffer manages an array in which messages are stored;
- the producer sends its messages to buffer;
- the consumer receives its messages from buffer.

In order to express the process buffer, non-deterministic choices have to be introduced. We must find a means for expressing the fact that the process buffer must execute either an input or an output command according to the circumstances:

- producer?mess is executed if the message buffer is not full and the producer has executed buffer!mess;
- consumer!mess is executed if the message buffer is not empty and the consumer has executed buffer?mess.

We shall not go into this further at the moment. We shall come back to it in Chapter 8, after having introduced the rendezvous and non-deterministic choice of the Ada language.

5.8 EXERCISES

5.8.1 Give a solution for the producer/consumer problem using events, with a buffer capacity of one message.

5.8.2 Same as Exercise 5.8.1 but with a buffer capacity of n events. (Hint: use an array of 2n events.)

5.8.3 Explain why the solution of Figure 5.7 (semaphores) is wrong if there are more than one of either producers or consumers. Modify the solution to deal with this possibility.
What about the monitor solution of Figure 5.6?

5.8.4 Solve the producer/consumer problem with the messages managed using a last-in first-out policy, so that the consumer always takes the message most recently produced. Use:

- monitors
- semaphores
- events (is it possible?).

5.8.5 Suppose the buffer holds only one message and the producer deposits its messages regardless of whether or not the previous message has been removed. Thus the producer is never blocked and some messages might be lost; the consumer always takes the last message produced but is blocked if the buffer is empty. Solve the problem using:

- monitors
- semaphores
- events.

5.8.6 Write a monitor that exports the procedures mail and receive (both having a parameter of type message) achieving the rendezvous semantics. Do the same using a module and:

- semaphores
- events.

5.8.7 Show how a mailbox can be used to implement a critical section.

Chapter 6

PORTAL AND MONITORS

In Portal [Businger 85] synchronization is expressed using monitors. The examples of monitors given in Chapter 5 have already used the syntax of Portal. Here we shall study more thoroughly certain points and describe an implementation of monitors. We will also show how interrupts are handled in the language and discuss its real-time features.

6.1 CLASSIC PROBLEMS SOLVED USING MONITORS

We shall return now to two problems that were solved in Chapter 4 using semaphores – the printer allocation problem and the readers/writers problem. From this discussion we will gain greater experience of monitors, and the second problem will illustrate the importance of the choice of the condition carried by a signal.

Let us come back first to the printers allocation problem. Figure 6.1 gives the monitor solution. It uses a monitor printers that exports two procedures, allocate and release.

```
monitor printers;
defines allocate, release;

  const
      m = ...; (* number of printers *)

  var
      nbr_free_printers: integer;
      allocated: array 1 .. n of boolean; (* gives state of each printer *)
      i: integer; (* see initialization code *)

  signal printer_free; (* propagates relation 'nbr_free_printers > 0' *)

  procedure allocate (var printer_no: integer);
  code
      if nbr_free_printers = 0 then printer_free.wait end if;
      (* when this line is reached there is at least one printer free; we now
         have to determine which one *)
```

```
      printer_no: = 1;
      while allocated[printer_no] do
        printer_no: = printer_no + 1;
      end while;
      allocated[printer_no]: = true;
      nbr_free_printers: = nbr_free_printers - 1;
    end allocate;

    procedure release (printer_no: integer);
    code
      allocated[printer_no]: = false;
      nbr_free_printers: = nbr_free_printers + 1;
      printer_free.send (* since nbr_free_printers > 0 *)
    end release;

  code (* initialization *)
    for i: = 1 to m do allocated[i]: = false end for;
    nbr_free_printers: = m;
  end printers;
```

Figure 6.1 **Monitor solution to the printers allocation problem**

This solution should be compared with that given in §4.5 (Figure 4.6). The two are in fact very similar. The semaphore free_printers of Figure 4.6 is replaced here by the signal printer_free and the integer variable nbr_free_printers. The signal printer_free carries the condition nbr_free_printers > 0.

Consider now the readers/writers problem with equal priorities (§4.6). Let us try to solve this problem using a single signal s. A first look suggests that we need the following variables:

- nbr_readers_waiting (for the signal s)
- nbr_writers_waiting (for the signal s)
- nbr_readers   (number of processes reading)
- nbr_writers   (at most one process)

We then write the procedure start_read as follows:

```
procedure start_read;
code
  if nbr_writers + nbr_writers_waiting > 0 then
    nbr_readers_waiting: = nbr_readers_waiting + 1;
    s.wait;
```

```
      nbr_readers_waiting: = nbr_readers_waiting – 1;
   end if;
   nbr_readers: = nbr_readers + 1;
end start_read;
```

This states that a reader must wait only if either writing is taking place or there is at least one writer waiting.

Similarly the procedure start_write can be expressed in this way:

```
procedure start_write;
code
   if nbr_writers + nbr_writers_waiting + nbr_readers +
      nbr_readers_waiting > 0
   then
      nbr_writers_waiting: = nbr_writers_waiting + 1;
      s.wait;
      nbr_writers_waiting: = nbr_writers_waiting – 1;
   end if;
   nbr_writers: = nbr_writers + 1
end start_write;
```

This states that a writer may start to write if and only if neither reading nor writing is taking place and there is neither a reader nor a writer waiting.

A problem arises in connection with the procedures finish_read and finish_write. How many processes must be awakened at the end of a write operation or of a read operation when nbr_readers = 0? If a writer is in front of the waiting queue of the signal s, then only one process has to be awakened and therefore s.send has to be executed only once. But if the queue starts with n readers then these n processes have to be awakened. How is this information to be found? The only possibility is to handle a queue explicitly, for example by using an array. This queue records each reader or writer having to wait and makes available the identities of all the processes waiting for the signal at any instant. However this is not very satisfactory if the queue is held in an array of fixed size as the total number of processes is not known. Anyway the above solution is not very elegant. This is due to the fact that the condition carried by the signal cannot be expressed in any simple manner.

The situation can be improved by introducing a second signal. Before explaining this we should note that the number of variables can be reduced, as follows:

- since we use only the expression nbr_writers + nbr_writers_waiting in the procedures start_read and start_write we can replace the two variables by the single variable total_writers, equal to the sum;

75

CONCURRENT PROGRAMMING

- the variable nbr_readers_waiting is useless. In the procedure start_read the condition nbr_readers_waiting > 0 can hold only if nbr_writers + nbr_writers_waiting > 0 – that is, only if total_writers > 0. So we can drop this variable without any effect on start_read.

The two signals required for the solution are:

- the signal no_reader which carries the condition nbr_readers = 0 (no reading is taking place);
- the signal no_writer which carries the condition nbr_writers = 0 (no writing is taking place).

The solution is given in Figure 6.2. The underlying idea is as follows. Suppose a writer is writing. The readers or writers that arrive will be blocked waiting for the signal no_writer (lines 11 and 23). A reader that is awakened will, before starting to read, awaken a second process (line 13). If this one too is a reader, it will in turn awaken a third, and so on until all the readers waiting in front of the signal's queue are awakened. The first writer to be awakened after a reader will be blocked again at the signal no_reader (line 24).

```
1    monitor readers_writers;
2    defines start_read, finish_read, start_write, finish_write;

3        var
4            nbr_readers: integer; (* number of processes that are reading *)
5            total_writers: integer; (* number writing or waiting to write *)

6        signal
7            no_reader; (* no process reading *)
8            no_writer; (* no process writing *)

9        procedure start_read;
10       code
11           if total_writers > 0 then no_writer.wait end if;
12           nbr_readers: = nbr_readers + 1;
13           no_writer.send;
14       end start_read;

15       procedure finish_read;
16       code
17           nbr_readers: = nbr_readers - 1;
18           if nbr_readers = 0 then no_reader.send end if;
```

76

```
19    end finish_read;

20    procedure start_write;
21    code
22        total_writers: = total_writers + 1;
23        if total_writers > 1 then no_writer.wait end if;
24        if nbr_readers > 0 then no_reader.wait end if;
25    end start_write;

26    procedure finish_write;
27    code
28        total_writers: = total_writers – 1;
29        no_writer.send;
30    end finish_write;

31    code (* initialization *)
32        nbr_readers: = 0;
33        total_writers: = 0
34    end readers_writers;
```

Figure 6.2 Monitor solution to the readers/writers problem (equal priorities)

The readers/writers problems with priority to the readers and priority to the writers respectively are left as an exercise (see 6.6.3 and 6.6.4). The solutions are simpler than the one we have just given. The reader should compare these solutions with the semaphore solutions obtained in Exercises 4.7.6 and 4.7.7, and also compare the semaphore and monitor solutions with the printers allocation problem (Exercises 4.7.4 and 6.6.1). This will illustrate the superiority of monitors over semaphores.

6.2   SEMANTICS OF MONITORS

We have already introduced, in §5.4, some of the elements of the semantics of monitors:

- at any time only one process can be executing within the monitor. This process is said to *occupy* the monitor and is its *active process*;
- when the active process executes the procedure *wait* it is blocked and the mutual exclusion on the monitor is released.
- when the active process executes the procedure *send* the process thus awakened becomes the new active process of the monitor.

However, these rules do not cover all the possibilities. Consider, for

77

example, the monitor readers_writers of Figure 6.2, and the following situation:

- a reader R1 and a writer W1 are waiting for the signal no_writer (lines 11, 23), with R1 at the front of the queue;
- writer W2 finishes writing, calls the procedure finish_write and sends the signal no_writer (line 29);
- reader R1, at the front of the queue, becomes the active process in the monitor and sends the signal no_writer (line 13);
- this wakes up writer W1 which now becomes the active process; but it is blocked again at the signal no_reader, since nbr_readers > 0 (line 24). Which process becomes the active one at this instant? Is it the reader R1 or the writer W2?

The complete semantics must specify precisely the active process in any situation. Although some details of the semantics can vary from one implementation to another, its core mentioned in §5.4 and recalled above is widely accepted.

In order to describe the semantics of Portal monitors, let's introduce the concept of the state of a process. The possible states with respect to a monitor m are the following:

- *activatable*: state of a process that can get the processor. In any monitor there can be only one process in this state. This characterizes the mutual exclusion property of the monitor. The term is more precise than active, used above, because it suggests that the process does not necessarily have the processor permanently (the processor being possibly shared among all the processes that may be executed);
- *stopped*: state of a process that can become activatable as soon as there are no more activatable processes in the monitor. We have to distinguish:

  — *entry-stopped*: state of a process that wishes to enter a monitor that is already occupied;
  — *send-stopped*: state of a process that is stopped having executed the procedure *send*;

- *waiting*: state of a process that is waiting for a signal;
- *outside*: state of a process that is not in the monitor, either after having left or before trying to enter. A process not in any of the previous states is in this state.

The state of a process will change after any of the following actions:
- *enter*: corresponding to the call of a procedure of the monitor;
- *wait*: corresponding to a call to the procedure wait;

- *send*: corresponding to a call to the procedure send;
- *leave*: corresponding to the completion of the execution of a monitor procedure.

We can now define the semantics by describing the change(s) that result from each action. These are given in Figure 6.3, in which the following notation is used:

(e) $\xrightarrow{\text{a}}$ (e') means that a process in state e changes to state e' on executing action a.

(e1,e2) $\xrightarrow{\text{a}}$ (e1',e2') means that if there is a process p2 in state e2, then a process p1, in state e1, executing action a causes a paired state change: process p1 changes from state e1 to e1' and p2 from e2 to e2'.

Figure 6.3 shows that a single action can trigger several state changes – for example, enter can lead to the changes given by rules A1 and A2. The ordering of the rules in Figure 6.3 is therefore significant: when an action can result in more than one state change it is the change given first in Figure 6.3 that occurs.

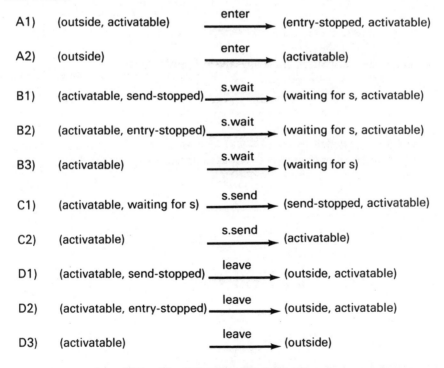

A1) (outside, activatable) $\xrightarrow{\text{enter}}$ (entry-stopped, activatable)

A2) (outside) $\xrightarrow{\text{enter}}$ (activatable)

B1) (activatable, send-stopped) $\xrightarrow{\text{s.wait}}$ (waiting for s, activatable)

B2) (activatable, entry-stopped) $\xrightarrow{\text{s.wait}}$ (waiting for s, activatable)

B3) (activatable) $\xrightarrow{\text{s.wait}}$ (waiting for s)

C1) (activatable, waiting for s) $\xrightarrow{\text{s.send}}$ (send-stopped, activatable)

C2) (activatable) $\xrightarrow{\text{s.send}}$ (activatable)

D1) (activatable, send-stopped) $\xrightarrow{\text{leave}}$ (outside, activatable)

D2) (activatable, entry-stopped) $\xrightarrow{\text{leave}}$ (outside, activatable)

D3) (activatable) $\xrightarrow{\text{leave}}$ (outside)

Figure 6.3   Semantics of Portal monitors

Consider first rules A1 and A2 which define the semantics of the entry into a monitor. Suppose a process p1 wishes to enter a monitor m. If m contains an activatable process then A1 applies, p1 changes to state entry-stopped and cannot therefore enter m. If, on the other hand, there is no activatable process in m then A2 applies, and p1 becomes the activatable process in m. Thus A1 and A2 define the monitor's mutual exclusion property.

Rules C1 and C2 define the semantics of send. Suppose p1 executes s.send. If a process p2 is waiting for signal s then C1 applies, p1 changes into state send-stopped, and the process thus awakened (here p2) becomes the activatable process of m. However, if there is no process waiting for s then rule C2 applies: the sending of the signal has no effect.

Rules B1, B2, B3 and D1, D2, D3 define what happens when the activatable process p1, either is blocked at a signal or leaves the monitor. If some process p2 is in state send-stopped then it becomes the activatable process, by rule B1 or D1; if not, then by rule B2 or D2 a process in state entry-stopped, if any, becomes the activatable process.

An important piece of information is missing in Figure 6.3, that is, how the choice is made when there are several candidates for the second process in the paired state changes of rules B1, B2, C1, D1, D2. For a given monitor m:

- the processes in the state entry-stopped are handled using a FIFO policy;
- the processes in the state send-stopped are handled using a LIFO (last-in first-out) policy;
- the processes waiting for a signal are handled using a FIFO policy.

We can illustrate these rules, and those of Figure 6.3, with the monitor readers_writers of Figure 6.2. We start from the situation where a reader R1 and a writer W1 are both waiting for the signal no_writer (lines 11 and 23). The ensuing sequence of events is shown in Figure 6.4, which gives the successive states of each process. Times t_0 to t_5 correspond to the following actions:

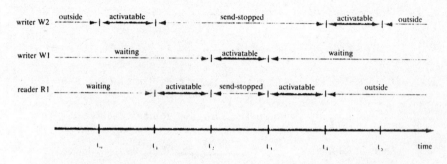

Figure 6.4   Changes of state of the processes for the monitor of Figure 6.2

- t_0: writer W2 calls procedure finish_write (Figure 6.2), rule A2 is applied;
- t_1: writer W2 executes no_writers.send (line 29), rule C1 is applied and reader R1, in front of the signal's queue, becomes activatable;
- t_2: reader R1 executes no_writer.send (line 13), rule C1 is applied and W1 becomes activatable;
- t_3: writer W1 is blocked at the signal no_reader (line 24), rule B1 is applied and R1 on top of the stack of send-stopped processes, becomes activatable again;
- t_4: reader R1 leaves the monitor, rule D1 is applied and W2 becomes activatable again;
- t_5: writer W2 leaves the monitor, rule D3 is applied.

The rules of Figure 6.3 implicitly cover the case of a process p calling a second monitor m2 from inside a first monitor m1. This call does not correspond to any action concerning m1 and therefore p continues to be the activatable process of m1 while executing in m2. This remains so even if process p is blocked at a signal in m2: a call in m2 to the procedure wait does not bring about any change of state for the process p in m1. However, unless treated with care, this can lead to deadlocks, as for example:

- a process p1 calls a monitor m1, and while in m1 calls another monitor m2 in which it is blocked at a signal s. Process p1 is still activatable in m1 but waiting in m2;
- a process p2 wishes to awaken p1. To do this it calls m1, from where it should call m2 in order to send the signal s.

This leads to a deadlock. Process p1 is waiting for the signal s which has to be sent by p2, but because p1 is occupying m1 it is preventing p2 from entering monitor m1, and consequently from entering m2 to send the signal.

6.3 PROGRAMMING INPUT/OUTPUT IN PORTAL

The Portal language does not define any procedure for either reading or writing. This is due to the fact that input and output can be expressed entirely at the level of device registers, and thus be programmed by the user.

We discussed the principles underlying the programming of input and output in Chapter 2. To implement this in a high-level language we must be able to:

- access the device registers
- handle interrupts.

In a computer like the PDP-11, having memory-mapped I/O, the device registers are accessed just as any other memory location. Access to these registers is therefore expressed as follows:

```
var dr_screen at 177564B: char; (* B indicates an octal number *)
```

81

The variable dr_screen (screen data register) allows the word at octal location 177564 to be addressed. Type char indicates that the content of this location is a character.

An interrupt is seen in Portal as a signal sent by a hidden process. A special clause in the declaration of a signal enables it to be linked to an interrupt vector. Such a signal is called an external signal. Declaration

signal interr_screen[64B];

means that an interrupt through the vector at octal address 64 will have the same effect as the execution of the procedure interr_screen.send. Thus the call interr_screen.wait causes the process to wait for the interrupt. Portal requires that when an interrupt arrives, one and only one process is waiting for the corresponding signal; an execution error is flagged if this is not the case. Loss of an interrupt can be symptomatic of a program error. The requirement that only one process is waiting for an external signal imposes a particular style of programming which is, after all, quite natural.

Consider now the writing of a character on a screen. Let's use the same peripheral interface as in Chapter 2:

- screen status register at octal address 177564
- screen data register at octal address 177566
- interrupt vector at octal address 64.

Recall that a value 1 for bit 7 of the status register means that the interface is ready to accept a character and that interrupt mode is enabled by setting bit 6 of this register.

Writing on the screen is shown in Figure 6.5. A monitor is used, because in Portal a signal has always to be declared within a monitor. The digits of the status register are manipulated by means of a set consisting of 16 elements (declared as type state, line 6). The compiler implements such a set using 16 bits, one for each element that could be included in the set. The presence of the i'th element is indicated by setting bit i, its absence by clearing bit i. Thus at line 15 the expression ready **not in** sr_screen is true if and only if the element ready is not in the set sr_screen – that is, if and only if bit 7 (see line 4) is 0. Further, state(interr) (lines 17, 20) stands for a constant of type state containing only element interr. This constant is represented by the following bit string:

15									6						0
0	0	0	0	0	0	0	0	0	1	0	0	0	0	0	0

The union (denoted by +) of sets state(interr) and sr_screen thus sets bit 6 of the screen status register, which enables the interrupt mode (line 17). The difference (denoted by –) of these sets clears bit 6 which disables the interrupt mode (line 20). If this were not done an interrupt would occur when the interface became ready again. This unexpected interrupt would result in an execution error.

```
1    monitor [4] screen;
2    defines write;

3        type
4          bits = (b0, b1, b2, b3, b4, b5, interr, ready, b8, b9
                    b10, b11, b12, b13, b14, b15);
6          state = set of bits;

7        var
8          sr_screen at 177564B: status; (* screen status register *)
9          dr_screen at 177566B: char; (* screen data register *)

10       signal
11         interr_screen[64B]; (* interrupt signal *)

12       procedure write(c: char);
13       (* write the character c on the screen *)

14       code
15         if ready not in sr_screen then
16         (* interface not ready *)
17           sr_screen: = sr_screen + state(interr);
18             (* sets interrupt bit *)
19           interr_screen.wait; (* waits for the interrupt *)
20           sr_screen: = sr_screen – state(interr);
21             (* clears interrupt bit *)
22         end if;
23         dr_screen: = c (* writes character c on the screen *)
24       end write;

25   end screen;
```

Figure 6.5   Portal program for writing a character on the screen

The number in brackets at line 1 of the monitor gives the priority of the *processor* during execution of the monitor. This is the same priority as the screen device interrupt (see §2.3). Thus as explained in Chapter 2, screen interrupts are masked in the monitor. This avoids unexpected interrupts, which could occur if the device status changed to ready between the test in line 15 and the wait for the interrupt in line 19.

The monitor of Figure 6.5 can be improved by adding a buffer (Figure 6.6). A process that calls write then places the character in the buffer without being aware of it and need not wait for the device to become ready. The monitor must now contain a process for copying the characters from the buffer to the screen. Notice that a process declared within a monitor is initially the activatable process of the monitor.

```
monitor [4] screen;
defines write;

    type
        bits = (b0, b1, b2, b3, b4, b5, interr, ready, b8, b9,
                b10, b11, b12, b13, b14, b15);
        state = set of bits;

    var
        sr_screen at 177564B: status; (* screen status register *)
        dr_screen at 177566B: char; (* screen data register *)

    signal
        interr_screen[64B]; (* interrupt signal *)

    const
        n = ...; (* buffer capacity *)

    var
        buffer: array 1 .. n of char;
        nbr_char: integer; (* number of characters in buffer *)
        inpt, outpt: 1 .. n; (* indices in array buffer *)

    signal
        nonfull, nonempty;

    procedure write (c: char);
        (* puts the character c in the buffer *)
    code
        if nbr_char = then (* buffer full *) nonfull.wait end if;
        buffer[inpt]: = c; (* puts the character in the buffer *)
        inpt: = inpt rem n + 1;
        nbr_char: = nbr_char + 1;
        nonempty.send
    end write;

    procedure get (var c: char);
    (* takes a character from buffer *)
```

```
code
  if nbr_char = 0 then nonempty.wait (* buffer empty *) end if;
  c: = buffer[outpt]; (* takes a character *)
  outpt: = outpt rem n + 1;
  nbr_char: = nbr_char – 1;
  nonfull.send;
end get;


process copy;
(* copies the buffer to the screen *)
  var c: char;
code
  loop
    get (c);
    if ready not in sr_screen then (* interface not ready *)
      sr_screen: = sr_screen + state(interr);
      interr_screen.wait; (* waits for the interrupt *)
      sr_screen: = sr_screen – state(interr);
    end if;
    dr_screen: = c; (* writes character c on the screen *)
  end loop;
end copy;

code (* initialization *)
  nbr_char: = 0;
  inpt: = 1; outpt: = 1;
end screen;
```

Figure 6.6 Writing a character on the screen using a buffer

Finally, Figure 6.7 gives the text of a monitor for both reading characters typed on the keyboard and writing on the screen. The keyboard (see Chapter 2) is characterized by:

- a status register at octal address 177560
- a data register at octal address 177562
- an interrupt vector at octal address 60.

The two main procedures are read_line and write_line, each having as parameter not a single character but a whole line of type **string** (a string of characters). This enables read_line to take account of an erase character.

To understand procedures read_line and write_line, the effects of sending

85

to the screen the codes for the following ASCII characters must be kept in mind (all codes are octal):

- NUL (ASCII code 0) has no effect;
- BELL (ASCII 7) gives an audible signal;
- BACK SPACE (ASCII 10), abbreviated to BS, moves the cursor one space to the left in the current line, without modifying any text;
- LINE FEED (ASCII 12), abbreviated to LF, moves the cursor down one line (no text modification);
- CARRIAGE RETURN (ASCII 15), abbreviated to CR, moves the cursor to the start of the current line (no text modification).

Monitor terminal of Figure 6.7 has the following features:

- when writing, a line must be terminated either by CARRIAGE RETURN or by NUL. After the line has been written CR returns the cursor to the start of the next line, NUL leaves it immediately to the right of the last character written;
- when reading, the end of a line is reached when a CR is read. Each line however has a maximum length, given by the predefined function length. A warning signal is sounded when this length is reached; only CR or BS is accepted after this warning. Use of BS enables the last character of the line to be deleted. To delete a character from the screen the sequence BS, SPACE, BS must be sent (see line 92 in Figure 6.7).

```
1    monitor [4] terminal;
2    defines write_line, read_line;

3        type
4            bits = (b0, b1, b2, b3, b4, b5, interr, ready, b8, b9,
                     b10, b11, b12, b13, b14, b15);
6            state = set of bits;

7        var
8            sr_keyboard at 177560B: state; (* keyboard status register *)
9            dr_keyboard at 177562B: char; (* keyboard data register *)
10           sr_screen   at 177564B: state; (* screen status register *)
11           dr_screen   at 177566B: char; (* screen data register *)

12       signal
13           interr_keyboard [60B],
14           interr_screen [64B]; (* interrupt signals *)
```

```
15   const
16      (* declaration of ASCII codes *)
17         NUL  = 0C; (* C indicates an octal constant of type char *)
18         BELL = 7C;
19         BS   = 10C; (* BACK SPACE *)
20         LF   = 12C; (* LINE FEED *)
21         CR   = 15C; (* CARRIAGE RETURN *)
22         SP   = 40C; (* SPACE *)
23      n = 100; (* buffer capacity *)

24   var
25      buffer: array 1 .. n of char;
26      nbr_char: integer;
27         (* number of characters in the buffer *)
28      inpt, outpt: 1 .. n; (* indices in the array buffer *)

29   signal
30      nonfull, nonempty;

31   procedure read (var c: char);
32   (* reads a character from keyboard *)
33   code
34      if ready not in sr_keyboard then
35      (* no character typed *)
36         sr_keyboard: = sr_keyboard + state(interr);
37         interr_keyboard.wait; (* waits for interrupt *)
38         sr_keyboard: = sr_keyboard - state(interr);
39      end if;
40      c: = dr_keyboard; (* reads the character *)
41      (* suppress here any parity bit *)
42   end read;

43   procedure put (c: char);
44   (* puts the character into the buffer *)
45   code
46      if nbr_char = n then (* buffer full *) nonfull.wait
47      end if;
48      buffer[inpt]: = c; (* puts character into buffer *)
49      inpt: = inpt rem n + 1;
50      nbr_char: = nbr_char + 1;
51      nonempty.send;
52   end put;
```

```
53    procedure get (var c: char);
54    (* gets a character from the buffer *)
55    code
56      if nbr_char = 0 then (* buffer empty *) nonempty.wait end if;
57      c: = buffer[outpt]; (* gets a character from buffer *)
58      outpt: = outpt rem n + 1;
59      nbr_char: = nbr_char − 1;
60      nonfull.send;
61    end get;

62    procedure write_line (line:string);
63    (* puts the characters of the string line into the buffer; a line is
         terminated by CR or NUL; CR starts a new line on the screen *)
64      var
65        i: integer;
66    code
67      i: = 0;
68      repeat
69        i: = i + 1;
70        put(line[i]);
71        if line[i] = CR then (* move to the next line *)
72          put(LF);
73        end if;
74      until (line[i] = CR) or (line[i] = NUL) or (i = length(line));
75        (* length (line) = length of the actual parameter *)
76    end write_line;

77    procedure read_line (var line: string);
78    (* reads a line and echoes the characters read, finishing when CR is
         read; the procedure takes the deletion character BS into
         account *)
79      var
80        i: integer;
81        c: char;
82    code
83      i: = 0;
84      repeat
85        read(c);
86        case c

87          of CR: i: = i + 1; line[i]: = c;
88            put(CR); put(LF); (* echo *)
```

```
89           of BS: if i > 0 then (* deletion of a character *)
90               i: = i - 1;
91               (* delete the character from the screen *)
92               put(BS); put(SP); put(BS);
93            end if;

94         else
95            if i = length (line) - 1 then put(BELL)
96               (* last character of the line must be CR; warn the user *)
97            else
98               i: = i + 1; line[i]: = c;
99               put(c); (* echo *)
100           end if;

101        end case;
102     until c = CR;
103  end read_line;

104  process copy; (* copies contents of the buffer to the screen *)
105     var c: char;
106  code
107     loop
108        get(c);
109        if ready not in sr_screen then (* interface not ready *)
110           sr_screen: = sr_screen + state(interr);
111           interr_screen.wait;
112           sr.screen: = sr.screen - state(interr);
113        end if;
114        dr_screen: = c (* writes character c *)
115     end loop
116  end copy;

117  code (* initialization *) nbr_char: = 0; inpt: = 1; outpt: = 1
118  end terminal;
```

Figure 6.7   Reading and writing lines of characters on a terminal

This monitor provides a satisfactory solution to the problem provided that there is no interference between calls to read_line and write_line – that is, provided no process calls write_line while another is executing read_line. There are several ways to handle possible interferences. One is to impose mutual exclusion on the two procedures, which requires a boolean variable and another signal. But this will not allow an urgent message to be displayed while a process is reading. If p1 is the process with the urgent message and p2 the reader we can proceed as follows:

- p2's reading is interrupted;
- p1 message is written, starting on a new line of the screen;
- characters of the current line already typed are displayed again;
- p2's reading is resumed.

A more general solution makes use of windows. The real screen is used to simulate a number of virtual screens, one of which is assigned to each process. No interference will occur between processes using different windows.

6.4 REAL-TIME FEATURES OF PORTAL

The Portal language enables us to take time into account either directly or indirectly:

- a process can wait for a signal, specifying a maximum waiting time;
- priorities can be assigned to different processes, and can consequently influence the processor allocation. This may help in satisfying time constraints.

Consider the following declarations:

```
var b: boolean;
    t: integer;
signal s;
```

Waiting for s with a delay is expressed:

```
s.wait (delay ==t, timeout =:b);
```

This call will block the process until the signal s is received but no longer than the delay t. How time is interpreted depends on the implementation, a typical case being that one unit of time corresponds to 20 ms. The actual parameter b is set to false if the waiting process is awakened after the signal s is sent, and to true if it is awakened by expiry of the specified delay. The delay is measured by counting interrupts from the system clock; a delay of t actually means a delay of between t-1 and t time units (see Figure 6.8).

The wait-with-delay mechanism can be useful when external information

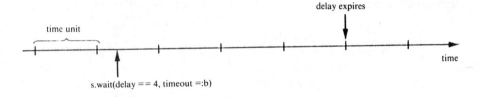

Figure 6.8   Wait with delay (time axis shows clock interrupts)

is expected, enabling a default option to be taken up if it does not arrive within some specified time, eg:

```
interrupt.wait(delay == ten_sec, timeout =:failure);
if failure then ...
```

Now consider the other real-time feature of Portal, the possibility of being able to assign priorities to processes. The number of priority levels will also depend on the implementation, a typical number being eight, with zero the lowest priority and seven the highest.

A priority is assigned to a process at the time of declaration, eg:

```
process [2] producer;
    ....
end producer;
```

This priority, shown here by [2], is called the *base priority* of the process. As we have seen in §6.3, a monitor also can be given a priority:

```
monitor [4] terminal;
    ....
end terminal;
```

When a process is being executed within a monitor it takes the priority of the monitor during this execution. This leads to the idea of a process's *current priority*. Initially the current priority is set to the process's base priority, but it may change as the process enters and leaves different monitors.

The default rules for priorities are:

- unless declared otherwise, the base priority of a process is 0;
- a process declared within a monitor is given the priority of the monitor;
- unless declared otherwise, the priority of a monitor is 3.

The (current) priority of a process is used in two distinct ways: one related to software, the other to hardware. The first concerns process scheduling. So long as a process of priority p is runnable – that is, is neither waiting nor in one of the stopped states (see §6.2) – no process of priority lower than p will be executed. The lower priority processes will be executed only when the processes of priority p are all either waiting or in one of the stopped states.

The hardware usage of priority is the following: when a process of priority p is being executed the processor is given the same priority. This explains why interrupts of priority less than or equal to p are masked when a process is executing within a monitor of priority p.

The last point to note is that a process of current priority p cannot call a monitor of priority less than p. Suppose a process executing in a monitor m1 of priority 5 could call a monitor m2 of priority 3. Monitor m1, of priority 5, would then be occupied by a process of priority 3, which could result in m1 not being released quickly enough. Any process of priority 4 or 5 would then be blocked outside of m1 by a process of priority 3.

For an illustration of the use of priorities, consider again the example of the terminal emulator (Figure 5.5). The corresponding Portal program has the structure given in Figure 6.9. This program consists of four processes and six monitors. Two monitors implement the buffers and four are concerned with the four sources of interrupts: the screen, the keyboard, transmission of characters to the host, and reception of characters from the host.

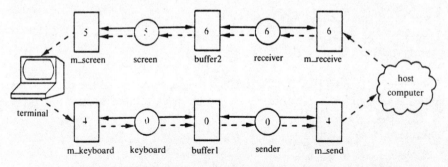

Figure 6.9 **Structure of a Portal program for terminal emulation (circle = process, rectangle = monitor, number = priority, full lines = monitor call, dotted lines = information flow)**

Process keyboard calls monitor m_keyboard to read a character typed on the keyboard and puts it in the monitor buffer1. Process sender takes a character from buffer1 and calls monitor m_send to transmit it to the host computer. Process receiver calls monitor m_receive to read a character sent by the host and puts it in buffer2. Finally, process screen takes a character from buffer2 and calls monitor m_screen to write it on the screen.

The critical part of this program is that concerned with receiving characters sent by the host, for these will be lost if process receiver cannot handle them quickly enough. There is no corresponding risk of losing characters typed on the keyboard, for even the fastest typing is very much slower than the hardware. Process receive, therefore, must have the highest priority. Process screen, in turn, must have priority over keyboard and sender so that it can empty buffer2 fast enough to ensure that process receiver is not blocked finding this buffer full.

Suppose now that all four interrupt sources have priority 4 (although the best arrangement would clearly be that interrupts on the line from the host to the PC had highest priority). The four monitors handling these interrupts must all have at least this priority to ensure the masking of interrupts. The other constraints to be satisfied are:

- no process of priority p must call a monitor of priority less than p;
- the current priorities of processes screen and receiver must always be higher than those of processes keyboard and sender, for the same reasons as those that led to the choice of the base priorities of the four processes.

Taking account of all these requirements leads to the priorities given in Figure 6.9.

6.5 MONITOR IMPLEMENTATION: THE PORTAL KERNEL

We shall now describe the kernel of the Portal language. To avoid unnecessary detail we shall consider only the essential features – that is, entering and leaving a monitor and the calls to procedures wait and send. We shall not discuss either the implementation of wait with delay or the handling of interrupts.

We will start with the data structure that is central to the kernel. This is an array called *display*, with an entry for each priority level (see Figure 6.10). Each entry is the head of a list of processes, the ith entry (typically $0 \leqslant i \leqslant 7$) being the head of the list of the ready processes of priority i. A process is said to be ready if it is executable – that is, either the activatable process in a monitor or a process outside any monitor. As Figure 6.10 shows, the display has one further entry, labelled –1 (the lowest priority being 0), and containing an idle process defined as being always ready. This guarantees that there is always at least one ready process, which simplifies the kernel programming by suppressing the need to consider special cases.

The display is used each time the kernel has to choose the next process to execute. It is scanned in decreasing order of priority and the process at the head of the first non-empty list is selected.

The Portal kernel handles processes, signals and monitors, so it needs to have access to information giving the states of these objects. For each object this information is contained in a descriptor: thus there are process descriptors, signal descriptors and monitor descriptors.

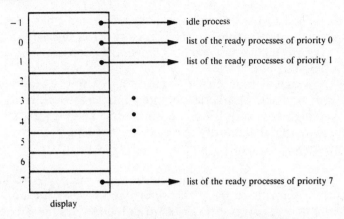

Figure 6.10 Display: one entry for each priority level

A process descriptor contains the following information:

- a double link to enable the process to be included in a list (for the sake of clarity, only a single link is shown in the figures below);
- a stack pointer (sp);
- the base priority of the process;
- the address of the descriptor of the monitor within which the process is at that instant. If the process is not in any monitor, this field is set to nil.

This is illustrated in Figure 6.11; processes p1 and p2 are ready at priority 4, p1 has base priority 0 and is in the monitor m.

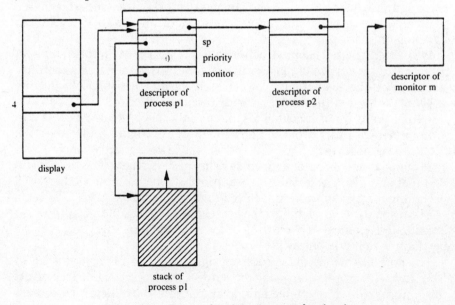

Figure 6.11 Process descriptor (sp = stack pointer)

94

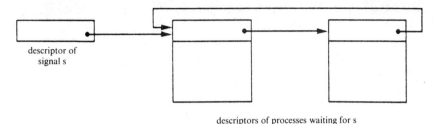

descriptor of
signal s

descriptors of processes waiting for s

Figure 6.12   Signal descriptor

A signal descriptor consists of a single field, containing the head of the list of processes waiting for the signal. Figure 6.12 shows two processes waiting for the signal s.

A monitor descriptor contains the following information:

- a flag showing the state of the monitor, occupied or free;
- the priority of the monitor;
- the head of the list of processes in either of the stopped states, with processes in send-stopped state preceding those in entry-stopped state.

It is perhaps surprising that a single list is enough to implement both the stopped states. This is because the send-stopped processes are managed in LIFO order, while the entry-stopped processes are managed in FIFO order. So, (1) a process that changes into the send-stopped state is pushed to the head of the list, (2) a process that changes into the entry-stopped state is added to the tail of the list, and (3) processes are always taken from the head of the list. Figure 6.13 shows an occupied monitor of priority 4, with two processes, in some stopped state (whether send-stopped or entry-stopped is indistinguishable).

We can now describe the four main procedures of the Portal kernel:

- enter, called on entry to a monitor
- leave, called when leaving a monitor
- wait
- send.

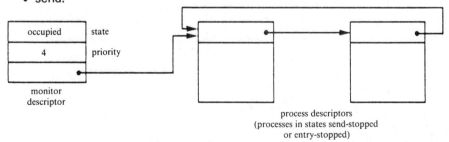

occupied	state
4	priority

monitor
descriptor

process descriptors
(processes in states send-stopped
or entry-stopped)

Figure 6.13   Monitor descriptor

95

Calls to the first two are generated by the compiler, so these procedures are not visible to the user. Suppose for example that a monitor m exports a procedure p:

```
procedure p;
code
    ...
end p;
```

The compiler will insert the necessary monitor calls, so the compiled code will be:

```
procedure p;
code
    enter (address of monitor descriptor);
    ...
    leave
end p;
```

Each of the four main procedures uses a procedure called next_process, by means of which the next active process (the process to be given control of the processor) is chosen:

```
procedure next_process;
code
    scan display in decreasing order of priority until a non-empty list is found;
    choose for execution the process at the head of this list;
end next_process;
```

Figure 6.14 shows the procedure enter, for entering a monitor.

```
procedure enter (new monitor: address of monitor descriptor);
code
    push the address of the current monitor on the process stack;
        (* this information will be used on leaving the monitor *)
    put the address of the new monitor in the process descriptor;
    if new monitor is free then new monitor becomes occupied;
        if current priority of process < priority of monitor then remove the
            process from the display;
            insert the process at the head of the display list corresponding to
            the priority of the monitor;
        end if
```

else remove the process from the display;
      insert the process at the tail of the list 'send-stopped/entry-stopped'
      of the new monitor;
      next_process;
   end if;
  end enter;

Figure 6.14   Procedure for entering a monitor

The entry into a monitor is illustrated in Figure 6.15 and 6.16. In Figure 6.15, process p1, at current priority 0, is not in any monitor. Figure 6.16 shows the situation after p1 has entered monitor m.

We next suppose that p1 executes the call s.wait. Figure 6.17 shows procedure wait, and Figure 6.18 the situation after execution of s.wait.

As Figure 6.18 shows, p2 is now the active process. Suppose p2 also calls m in order to execute s.send. Procedure send is given in Figure 6.19 and the new situation after s.send has been executed is shown in Figure 6.20.

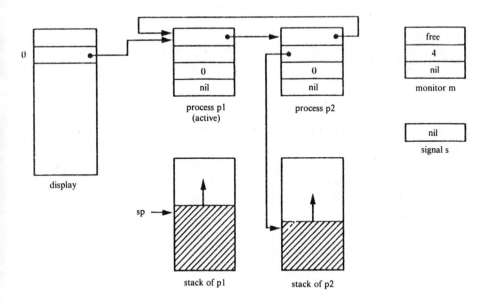

Figure 6.15   Situation before entry to a monitor: currently active process p1 wishes to enter monitor m

97

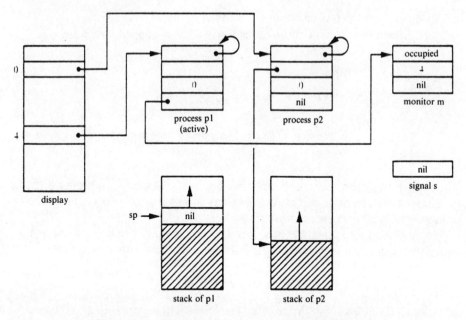

Figure 6.16   Situation after process p1 has entered monitor m

procedure wait(s: address of signal descriptor);
code
   (∗ the descriptor of the current monitor can be accessed via the process
     descriptor ∗)
   remove the process from the display;
   put the process at the tail of the waiting list of signal s;
   if list 'send-stopped/entry-stopped' of the current monitor is empty **then**
     current monitor becomes free
   else take the process at the head of the list 'send-stopped/entry-stopped'
      of the current monitor;
     insert this process at the head of the display list corresponding
     to the priority of the monitor; (∗ this will become the next active
     process ∗)
   end if;
   next_process;
end wait;

Figure 6.17   Implementation of procedure wait

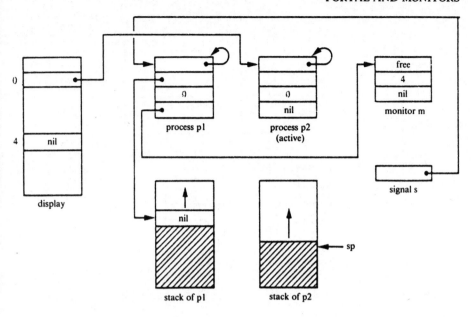

Figure 6.18   Situation after execution of s.wait by process p1 (p2 is the active process)

procedure send(s: address of signal descriptor);
code
  (∗ the descriptor of the current monitor can be accessed via the
    process descriptor ∗)
  if list of processes waiting for the signal s is not empty
  then take the process at the head of this waiting list (call it the
      awakened process);
    remove the current process (the process that executes send) from the
      display;
    insert the current process at the head of the 'send-stopped/entry-
      stopped' list of the current monitor;
    put the awakened process at the head of the display list corresponding
      to the priority of the monitor (∗ this will be the next active process ∗);
    next_process;
  end if;
end send;

Figure 6.19   Implementation of procedure send

Finally, p1 leaves monitor m. The procedure is given in Figure 6.21 and the
situation after leaving in Figure 6.22.

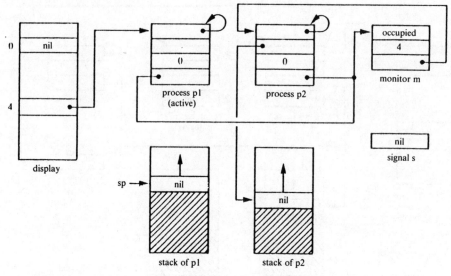

Figure 6.20   Situation after execution of s.send by process p2 (p1 is the active process)

procedure leave;
  code
    (* the descriptor of the current monitor can be accessed via the
      process descriptor *)
    remove the process from the display;
    if list 'send-stopped/entry-stopped' of the current monitor is empty
    then
      the current monitor becomes free;
    else take the process at the head of the list 'send-stoped/entry-stopped'
        of the current monitor;
      put this process at the head of the display list corresponding
      to the priority of the monitor (* this will be the next active process *)
    end if;
    pop the address of a monitor descriptor from the stack of the process
      leaving the monitor (* this address was pushed on entry into the
      monitor *)
    if this descriptor address is nil
    then (* the process is outside any monitor *) insert the process at the tail
      of the display list corresponding to the process's base priority;
    else insert the process at the tail of the display list
      corresponding to the priority of the monitor in which it is now;
    end if;
    next_process;
  end leave;

Figure 6.21   Implementation of procedure leave

100

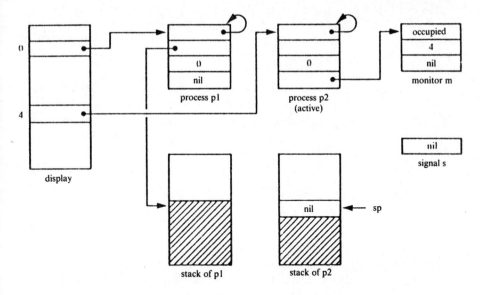

Figure 6.22   Situation after process p1 has left monitor m (process p2 is active)

We have not discussed here process switching caused by interrupts. It is, however, worth saying a few words about the particular case of time-slicing, ie process switching caused by the system clock. This can be described by the following procedure:

```
procedure time_slicing;
    (* called after each clock interrupt *)
code
    remove the active process from the head of the display;
    queue the process on tail of the same display list;
    next_process;
end time_slicing;
```

For efficiency reasons Portal implementations perform time-slicing only between processes of priority 0 (and in some cases, even not at all). The reason for this is that it is usual to assign the lowest priority to compute-bound processes (usually a unique process in a program) and to assign higher priorities to I/O bound processes.

101

6.6 EXERCISES

6.6.1 Give a monitor solution for the problem of Exercise 4.7.4 (allocation of printers when a process can request either one or two printers).

6.6.2 Consider two types of resources R1 and R2 (eg printers and magnetic tape drives), with N1 and N2 units available respectively. Write a monitor for managing these resources, assuming that each process can request:

either   one unit of R1
or   one unit of R2
or   one unit each of R1 and R2.

The solution must satisfy the following conditions:

- if a process requests both R1 and R2 this will not be granted unless at least one unit of each is free;
- priority is given to processes requesting one unit each of R1 and R2.

6.6.3 Give a monitor solution for the problem of readers and writers, with priority to the readers.

6.6.4 Same as Exercise 6.6.3 but with priority to the writers.

6.6.5 Write a monitor terminal that allows writing during reading. Solve the problem in the following way (see §6.3):

- stop the reading
- perform the writing
- redisplay the characters of the current line already typed
- resume the reading.

6.6.6 Add the implementation of interrupt handling to the Portal kernel. Assume that an interrupt causes a call to a procedure interrupt_send.

6.6.7 Add the implementation of 'wait with delay' to the Portal kernel.

Chapter 7

MODULA-2 AND KERNELS

The language Modula-2 [Wirth 85] has no built-in mechanisms for mutual exclusion or synchronization. Instead, it provides the user with means for constructing such mechanisms for him or herself in the way he or she considers best suited to the problem in hand. To risk an analogy with tailoring, we might say that Portal (and Ada also) correspond to off-the-peg and Modula-2 to made-to-measure! This feature of Modula-2 derives from its quasi-parallel execution scheme.

7.1 CREATING PROCESSES

Modula-2 does not provide processes as syntactic units; there is no reserved word such as **process** or any equivalent. A process is created in this language by a call to the procedure NEWPROCESS. Thus the number of processes in a Modula-2 program is not determined statically – that is, it is not known at compile time.

The procedure NEWPROCESS is exported from the standard module SYSTEM. This module exports several types, such as ADDRESS and PROCESS which we shall describe later, and procedures that allow low-level operations. We shall use several of the possibilities offered by this module, our aim in this chapter being to show how to write a kernel in Modula-2, which corresponds to using low-level operations to construct high-level tools.

The procedure NEWPROCESS has four parameters:

```
PROCEDURE NEWPROCESS (P: PROC; A: ADDRESS; n: CARDINAL;
                      VAR p1: PROCESS);
```

- P is a procedure that has no parameter (shown by the type PROC). This procedure constitutes the code of the process. A Modula-2 program terminates when any one of its processes reaches the final END in the procedure that constitutes its code.
- A and n define the process workspace. A is the process stack's base address and n its size (the type CARDINAL indicates a non-negative integer). The user has, therefore, to decide the size of stack that will be needed, in contrast to Portal where this is done by the compiler. Further, this workspace must be allocated before the call to

NEWPROCESS. Some implementations include a module Storage that exports a procedure ALLOCATE for this purpose.
- p1, of type PROCESS[1], is used to designate the process created. This is essential for the subsequent execution of the process, for NEWPROCESS only creates a process and does not activate it.

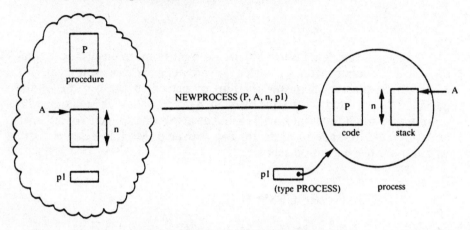

Figure 7.1   The procedure NEWPROCESS

Figure 7.1 illustrates the effect of NEWPROCESS. At the same time this diagram introduces an abstract graphical representation of a process that is independent of any implementation and which we shall use later to explain process switching. One possible implementation corresponding to this abstraction is given in Figure 7.2:

- the variable p1 holds the base address of the process stack;
- the bottom of the stack is used to save the stack pointer[2];
- the contents of the program counter (the register containing the address of the next instruction to be executed) can be saved on the stack. Initially the program counter will contain the address of the first instruction of the procedure P which constitutes the process code.

7.2   PROCESS SWITCHING

A process created by NEWPROCESS is not executed automatically: the execution must be asked for explicitly. Besides, a process once it has started to execute will not lose the processor unless it requests this explicitly (let's

---

[1] PROCESS has been deleted from the June 1984 revision of the language [Wirth 84]; the type ADDRESS must be used instead.
[2] In some implementations p1 is used directly to save the stack pointer.

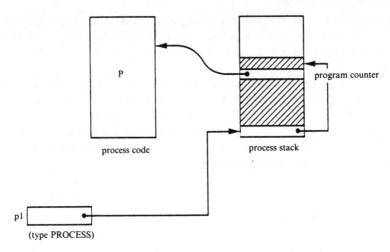

process code

process stack

program counter

P

pl

(type PROCESS)

Figure 7.2 Implementation of the type PROCESS

ignore interrupts for the moment). Here we have a fundamental difference from Portal (see §3.2):

- in Portal the kernel assigns the processor to different processes without any action on the part of the user; this is what is called pseudo-parallel execution.
- Modula-2 does not have a kernel and therefore is not in charge of sharing the processor among different processes: process switching must be programmed. This is what we have called quasi-parallel execution. A quasi-parallel process is often called a coroutine.

Thus in Modula-2 a process executes until it decides to give up the processor, and it then indicates which process is to be executed next. This switching is done using the procedure TRANSFER, also exported from module SYSTEM:

PROCEDURE TRANSFER (VAR p1, p2: PROCESS);

active

pl

p2

TRANSFER (p1, p2)
(executed by the
active process)

pl

p2

active

Figure 7.3 Representation of the procedure TRANSFER

This procedure suspends the executing process and activates process p2. After TRANSFER has been executed, p1 will identify the suspended process, and so make its resumption possible by a subsequent call to TRANSFER (see Figure 7.3).

Figure 7.4 illustrates the ideas we have been developing up to this stage. It shows a program consisting of four processes, three of which are created by calls to NEWPROCESS and the fourth being the initialization code of the main module. Figure 7.5 shows the switchings resulting from calls to TRANSFER. In this example p1 always designates the process that executes procedure X, p2 that for Y and p3 for Z.

```
MODULE Example;

FROM SYSTEM IMPORT
    PROCESS, TRANSFER, NEWPROCESS;
    (* importations from module SYSTEM *)

VAR pp, p1, p2, p3: PROCESS;

. . .
```

```
        PROCEDURE X;
        BEGIN
          LOOP

            . . .
(1)         TRANSFER (p1, p2);
            . . .
          END
        END X;
```

```
        PROCEDURE Y;
        BEGIN
          LOOP

            . . .
(2)         TRANSFER (p2, p3);
            . . .
          END
        END Y;
```

```
PROCEDURE Z:
BEGIN
  LOOP

    . . .

    TRANSFER (p3, p1);

    . . .

  END
END Z;
```

(3)

BEGIN (* initialization code *)

NEWPROCESS(X, . . , . . , p1);
NEWPROCESS(Y, . . , . . , p2);
NEWPROCESS(Z, . . , . . , p3);
(4)   TRANSFER(pp, p1)
END Example.

Figure 7.4   An example of process creation and process switch (see also Figure 7.5)

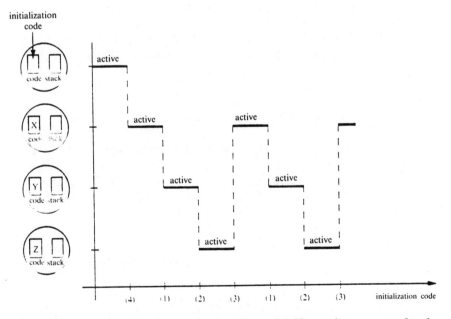

Figure 7.5   Process switches in the example of Figure 7.4. The numbers correspond to the different calls of TRANSFER

107

7.3   A KERNEL IMPLEMENTING SEMAPHORES

It is not advisable to use TRANSFER directly in a program. This would result in a badly structured and difficult to understand program. It is better to use the procedure TRANSFER inside a kernel to implement the synchronization mechanisms described in Chapters 4 and 5 – semaphores, monitors, mailboxes etc. As an exampale we now will a kernel that implements semaphores.

A kernel is usually provided in the form of a separately compiled module. Such a module is made up of two parts:

- a *definition part* that defines the exported objects. Here, these will be the type Semaphore and the procedures P, V, InitSemaphore, CreateProcess and StartSystem (see Figure 7.8);
- an *implementation part*, constituting the body of the module. Here this will contain the definition of the type Semaphore, the bodies of the procedures and the data structures handled by the kernel (see Figure 7.9).

Since the definition of the type Semaphore is given in the implementation part of the module and not in the definition part, the details of the type Semaphore are not known outside the kernel. The exportation of the type Semaphore is said to be opaque; a process can only manipulate a semaphore through the procedures P and V. Notice that opaque exportation is essentially limited to pointers.

The data structures handled by the kernel are shown in Figure 7.6. These are process descriptors and semaphore descriptors. A process descriptor has two fields:

- a link by means of which the process can be inserted into a list;
- a field of type PROCESS, for designating the process.

A process is always in one of the two following lists:

- the ready list. The variable Ready is the head of this list and the active process is always the one at the head of this list;
- the waiting list of a semaphore.

For simplicity we have omitted here any pointers to the end of the lists – this could however improve performance in cases where there are a great number of processes.

Given the data structures of Figure 7.6, the procedures P and V are easily implemented. To block a process (procedure P) only the following have to be done:

- take the process descriptor at the head of the list of ready processes and

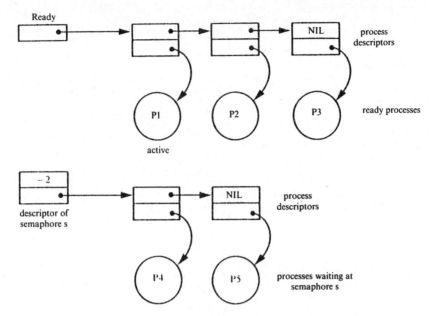

Figure 7.6   Data structures of the kernel implementing semaphores

put it at the end of the waiting queue of the semaphore;
- execute procedure TRANSFER to activate another process.

Figure 7.7 shows the situation following that of figure 7.6 when the active process is blocked after executing P; the shaded areas contain the parameters of TRANSFER.

To release a blocked process (procedure V) the descriptor of the process is taken from the list waiting at the semaphore and put at the end of the queue of 'ready' processes. The decision to put it at the tail rather than the head of this queue is not mandatory: nothing is imposed by the semantics of semaphores, and the choice is left to the implementor.

This kernel does not only define the procedures P, V or InitSemaphore (this last for initializing a semaphore) but also the procedures CreateProcess and StartSystem. Process creation is the task of the kernel alone and requires access to the kernel's data structures. The procedure CreateProcess allocates memory for the process descriptor and stack, then, using NEWPROCESS, creates the process and finally puts the descriptor at the end of the queue of 'ready' processes. The newly-created process is not yet active; activation will be done by the procedure StartSystem, which can be called, for example, from the initialization code of the main module after all the processes have been created: this is shown in Figure 7.10.

A difference from the Portal kernel of §6.5 is that here we have not defined an Idle process. The reason is that we have not yet provided for interrupt handling by the kernel. It is only when considering interrupts that a situation

109

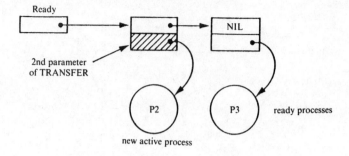

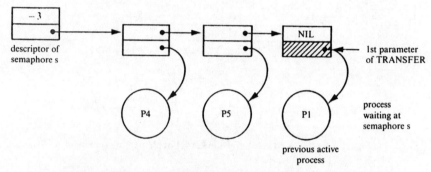

Figure 7.7 Process switching by the procedure p

can arise in which no process is ready yet there is no deadlock – there can be processes waiting for an interrupt. It is then sensible to introduce an Idle process which is always 'ready'. With the kernel we have described so far there is in fact a deadlock – and therefore an error – if no process is ready.

```
DEFINITION MODULE SemaphoreKernel1;

EXPORT QUALIFIED Semaphore, P, V, CreateProcess, StartSystem;

  TYPE Semaphore; (* opaque export *)

  PROCEDURE P (VAR s: Semaphore);

  PROCEDURE V (VAR s: Semaphore);

  PROCEDURE InitSemaphore (VAR s: Semaphore; n: INTEGER);
    (* n is the initial value of the semaphore *)

  PROCEDURE CreateProcess (P:PROC; StackSize:CARDINAL):
    (* creates a process that executes procedure P; the second parameter
      gives the size of the process stack needed *)
```

110

```
PROCEDURE StartSystem;
   (* called when all the processes have been created, initiates
      execution of first process *)


END SemaphoreKernel1.
```

Figure 7.8   Definition part of SemaphoreKernel1

```
IMPLEMENTATION MODULE SemaphoreKernel1;

FROM SYSTEM IMPORT ADDRESS, PROCESS, NEWPROCESS, TRANSFER;

FROM Storage IMPORT ALLOCATE;

   TYPE
     PtPrssDescr = POINTER TO ProcessDescr;

     ProcessDescr = RECORD
                       next: PtPrssDescr; (* next in the list of processes *)
                       prss: PROCESS (* to identify the process *)
                     END;
     SemaphoreDescr = RECORD
                       n: INTEGER;
                       waiting: PtPrssDescr (* head of list of
                                                waiting processes *)
                     END;

     Semaphore = POINTER TO SemaphoreDescr;
       (* opaque export is restricted to pointers *)

   VAR
     Ready: PtPrssDescr;
       (* head of the list of ready processes; the active process is always
          at the head of this list *)

PROCEDURE RemoveHead (VAR list: PtPrssDescr); VAR removed:
                        PtPrssDescr);
   (* takes the process at the head of the list *)
BEGIN
   removed: = list;
   IF list # NIL THEN list: = list↑.next END
END RemoveHead;
```

111

```
PROCEDURE InsertTail (VAR list: PtPrssDescr; toBeInserted: PtPrssDescr);
    (* puts the process toBeInserted at the tail of the list *)
  VAR p: PtPrssDescr;
BEGIN
  IF list = NIL THEN list: = toBeInserted
  ELSE p: = list;
        WHILE p↑.next NIL DO p: = p↑.next END;
        p↑.next: = toBeInserted;
  END;
  toBeInserted↑.next: = NIL;
END InsertTail;

PROCEDURE P(VAR s: Semaphore);
  VAR blocked: PtPrssDescr;
BEGIN
    s↑.n: = s↑.n – 1;
    IF s↑.n < 0 THEN (* block the process *);
      RemoveHead (Ready, blocked); (* remove process from ready list *)
      InsertTail(s↑.waiting, blocked);
        (* put the process at the tail of the semaphore's list *)
      IF Ready = NIL THEN HALT (* no process ready: deadlock *)
        ELSE TRANSFER (blocked↑.prss, Ready↑.prss);
            (* the process at the head of Ready list becomes active *)
      END;
    END;
END P;

PROCEDURE V(VAR s: Semaphore);
  VAR awakened: PtPrssDescr;
BEGIN
  s↑.n: = s↑.n + 1;
  IF s↑.n ≤ 0 THEN (* at least one process waiting *)
    RemoveHead(s↑.waiting, awakened);
      (* remove process at head of semaphore's list *)
    InsertTail (Ready, awakened);
      (* put process at tail of the Ready list *);
  END
END V;

PROCEDURE InitSemaphore (VAR s: Semaphore; n: INTEGER);
BEGIN NEW(s);
        s↑.n: = n; s↑.waiting: = NIL;
END InitSemaphore;
```

112

```
PROCEDURE CreateProcess (P: PROC; StackSize: CARDINAL);
(* creates a process and puts it at the tail of the Ready list *)
   VAR created: PtPrssDescr; a: ADDRESS;
BEGIN
   NEW(created);
      (* allocate memory for the process descriptor *)
   ALLOCATE (a, StackSize);
      (* allocate memory for the process stack *)
   NEWPROCESS (P, a, StackSize, created↑.prss);
   InsertTail (Ready, created);
END CreateProcess;


PROCEDURE StartSystem;
(* called after all processes have been created; initiates
   execution of the first process of the Ready list *)
   VAR init:PROCESS;
           (* to designate the process calling StartSystem *)
BEGIN IF Ready = NIL THEN HALT (* no process has been created *)
   ELSE TRANSFER (init, Ready↑.prss);
   END;
END StartSystem;


BEGIN (* initialization code *)
   Ready: = NIL
END SemaphoreKernel1.
```

Figure 7.9   Implementation part of SemaphoreKernel1

```
MODULE Example;
FROM SemaphoreKernel1 IMPORT Semaphore, P, V, InitSemaphore,
                                CreateProcess, StartSystem;
   VAR s: Semaphore;


PROCEDURE P1;
....
END P1;

....
PROCEDURE Pn;
...
END Pn;
```

```
BEGIN (* initialization code *)
  InitSemaphore (s, 0);
  CreateProcess (P1, ... ); ...; CreateProcess (Pn, ... );
  StartSystem;
END Example.
```

Figure 7.10   Example of use of SemaphoreKernel1

7.4   INPUT/OUTPUT PROGRAMMING AND INTERRUPTS

The same concepts concerning input/output prevail in Portal and Modula-2: neither has built-in procedures for input/output, but each makes it possible for appropriate procedures to be written in the language itself. In Modula-2 as in Portal the device registers can be accessed and the interrupts handled by the programmer.

Consider the case of a machine whose device registers are addressed just as any other memory locations – what is called memory-mapped I/O. Access to one of these registers is made by declaring a variable at an absolute address:

```
VAR ScreenReg[177564B]: CHAR;
```

The only difference with Portal is the use of square brackets to indicate an absolute address. In the case of a machine whose device registers are accessed using special instructions, Modula-2 will provide special procedures that correspond to these instructions.

Interrupt handling is a more serious problem. By its very nature, an interrupt can arise at any moment and must activate the process responsible for handling it. This process switch is therefore outside the control of the active process, which represents a departure from the quasi-parallel execution scheme. Interrupts constitute the only pseudo-parallel aspect of Modula-2. Waiting for an interrupt is expressed using the procedure IOTRANSFER, exported from the module SYSTEM:

```
PROCEDURE IOTRANSFER (VAR p1, p2: PROCESS; va:CARDINAL);
```

The third parameter, va, is the address of an interrupt vector. The call IOTRANSFER(p1, p2, va) is equivalent to the sequence

- TRANSFER(p1, p2);
- when an interrupt using vector va occurs, execute TRANSFER(p2, p1);

Thus IOTRANSFER suspends the active process until the interrupt occurs. The procedure is difficult to understand at first sight, because the parameter p2 plays two distinct roles: it first designates the process that gets the processor after execution of IOTRANSFER, and later the process that is suspended when the interrupt occurs; these two are not necessarily the same process. It would perhaps have been more sensible to use three parameters of type PROCESS.

It is good practice to use IOTRANSFER only inside a kernel. We shall return to this in the next section. For the moment let us study the little example of Figures 7.11 and 12, so as to get familiar with IOTRANSFER. It consists of a module that computes the time, using a device that produces interrupts at a fixed interval – a typical case would be every 20 ms. This device is characterized as follows:

- device register at address 177546B
- interrupt vector at address 100B
- to enable interrupts, bit 6 of the device register has to be set.

The module is called Clock (see Figure 7.12). The procedure Initialize creates a clock process and switches to it to enable interrupts. The type BITSET used here, allows the manipulation of specific bits of a word. Once interrupts are enabled, the clock process switches back to the process called Initialize. The clock process becomes active again at every interrupt using the vector 100B, and increments the time by one unit (20 ms). The number 7 in the module implementation part defines the priority of the processor during the execution of any process inside the module. This is the highest priority and ensures that all other interrupts are masked inside module Clock.

```
DEFINITION MODULE Clock;
EXPORT QUALIFIED Initialize, Time;
   VAR Time: ...;
   PROCEDURE Initialize;
END Clock.
```

Figure 7.11 Definition part of module Clock

```
IMPLEMENTATION MODULE Clock[7];

FROM SYSTEM IMPORT ADDRESS, PROCESS, NEWPROCESS, TRANSFER,
                   IOTRANSFER;

FROM Storage IMPORT ALLOCATE:

CONST
   ClockVector = 100B; (* address of Clock interrupt vector *)
   interr = 6; (* bit no of device register, used to enable clock interrupts *)
   ClockStackSize = 250; (* size of stack for clock process *)
```

```
VAR
  ClockPrss, p: PROCESS;
  ClockReg[177546B]: BITSET; (* clock status register *)

PROCEDURE ClockCode; (* code for clock process *)
BEGIN Time: = ...; (* set Time to zero *)
  INCL(ClockReg, interr); (* sets interrupt bit, thus enabling interrupts *)
  LOOP
    IOTRANSFER(ClockPrss, p, ClockVector); (* suspend clock process,
                                              awaiting interrupt *)
    increment variable Time by one unit; (* on PDP-11 = 20 ms *)
  END
END ClockCode;

PROCEDURE Initialize; (* creates the clock process and enables it to do
                          initializations *)
  VAR a: ADDRESS;
BEGIN ALLOCATE(a, ClockStackSize); (* allocates memory for stack *)
  NEWPROCESS (ClockCode, a, ClockStackSize, ClockPrss);
  TRANSFER (p, ClockPrss); (* enables clock process to do
                              initializations *)
  END Initialize;
END Clock.
```

Figure 7.12   Implementation part of module Clock

7.5   A KERNEL PROVIDING SEMAPHORES AND HANDLING INTERRUPTS

We can now complete the kernel given in §7.3 by incorporating interrupt handling. This has to be done by the kernel because it involves process switching. The new kernel, given in Figures 7.14–15, has other new features:

- processes can be given priorities
- process switching is done at each clock interrupt
- an Idle process is introduced.

The introduction of the Idle process simplifies the writing of a kernel that includes interrupt handling: this ensures that there is always at least one process in the ready state. The Idle process should be active only if no other process is ready, and this consideration leads to the introduction of priorities. Here we provide a range of 9 levels, from a lowest of –1 to a highest of 7, with –1 reserved for Idle. Thus the kernel will have 9 ready lists,

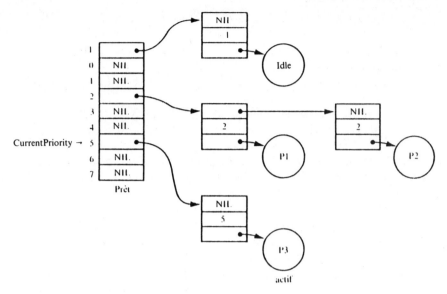

Figure 7.13 Process descriptors and ready lists (one for each priority level)

one for each priority level. The active process is always the one at the head of the non-empty list of highest priority, which is indicated by the variable CurrentPriority. The priority of each process is stored in an extra field in the descriptor, as shown in Figure 7.13. When a blocked process is awakened by execution of procedure V, this field is used to decide in which ready list to insert the process.

When a process has to wait for an interrupt it calls the procedure WaitInterr (see Figure 7.15), passing as a parameter the address of the interrupt vector. The wait is implemented as follows:

- the process is removed from the 'CurrentPriority' ready list;
- the kernel determines which process to execute next:
- the procedure IOTRANSFER is executed, causing the wait.

When the interrupt occurs the waiting process is reinserted at the head of the ready list corresponding to its priority; it becomes the active process provided that the interrupted process is not of higher priority. An illustration of the use of procedure WaitInterr is given in Figure 7.16.

In addition, we have provided in the new kernel time-slicing for processes of priority 0. As stated in §6.5, this is provided in some implementations of Portal. Here the procedure TimeSlice (see Figure 7.15), called at the end of procedure StartSystem, enables the clock and then waits for the interrupts. Then at each interrupt:

- the active process (call it p1) is suspended and the process that called

117

StartSystem is reactivated (call it p2). Normally, as in Figure 7.10, p2 is the process executing the initialization code of the main module;
- by a call to IOTRANSFER, p2 waits for a new interrupt, while reactivating either p1, if it is of priority > 0, or else the process at the head of the priority-0 ready list. In the second event p1 is put at the end of this list.

Let us say a final word about process Idle. This process consists of a loop in which the only instruction is a call to the procedure LISTEN, exported from SYSTEM, which reduces the priority of the processor to a level at which all interrupts are allowed. If this were not done, Idle would be executed at the priority of the module, ie 7, at which all interrupts are masked.

```
DEFINITION MODULE SemaphoreKernel2;
EXPORT QUALIFIED Semaphore, P, V, WaitInterr, CreateProcess,
                 StartSystem;

    TYPE Semaphore;

    PROCEDURE P(VAR s: Semaphore);

    PROCEDURE V(VAR s: Semaphore);

    PROCEDURE InitSemaphore (VAR s: Semaphore; n: INTEGER);
    (* n is the initial value of the semaphore *)

    PROCEDURE WaitInterr (vector: CARDINAL);
    (* suspends the calling process, waiting for an interrupt using the vector
       given as parameter *)

    PROCEDURE CreateProcess (P: PROC; StackSize: CARDINAL; priority:
                             INTEGER);
    (* creates a process that executes procedure P; the second parameter
       gives the size of the stack needed, the third the priority of the process *)

END SemaphoreKernel2.
```

Figure 7.14   Definition part of SemaphoreKernel2, a kernel handling interrupts

```
IMPLEMENTATION MODULE SemaphoreKernel2 [7];
FROM SYSTEM IMPORT ADDRESS, PROCESS, NEWPROCESS, TRANSFER,
                   IOTRANSFER, LISTEN;

FROM Storage IMPORT ALLOCATE;
```

```
CONST MinPriority = 0; MaxPriority = 7; (* range of process priorities; Idle
                                           has (MinPriority – 1) *)


TYPE
   TPriority = [MinPriority–1 .. MaxPriority];

   PtPrssDescr        = POINTER TO PrssDescr;

   PrssDescr          = RECORD
                           next: PtPrssDescr; (* next in the list of processes *)
                           prss: PROCESS; (* to designate the process *)
                           priority: TPriority; (* priority of the process *)
                        END;

   SemaphoreDescr = RECORD
                        n: INTEGER;
                        waiting: PtPrssDescr; (*head of list of waiting
                                                        processes *)
                     END;

   Semaphore = POINTER TO SemaphoreDescr; (* opaque export restricted
                                              to pointers *)
VAR
   Ready: ARRAY TPriority OF PtPrssDescr;
      (* heads of lists of ready processes, one list for each priority level *)

   CurrentPriority: TPriority;
      (* priority of the active process; this process is always that at the head
       of the list Ready[CurrentPriority] *)

   IdleCreation: BOOLEAN;
      (* true during the creation of process Idle *)

   i: TPriority; (* see initialization code at end *)


PROCEDURE RemoveHead(VAR list: PtPrssDescr; VAR removed:
                        PtPrssDescr);
(* removes the process at the head of the list *)
BEGIN removed: = list;
   IF list # NIL THEN list: = list↑.next END;
END RemoveHead;
```

119

```
PROCEDURE InsertHead (VAR list: PtPrssDescr; toInsert: PtPrssDescr);
(* puts the process toInsert at the head of the list *)
BEGIN toInsert↑.next: = list;
   list: = toInsert;
END InsertHead;

PROCEDURE InsertTail(VAR list: PtPrssDescr; toInsert: PtPrssDescr);
(* puts the process toInsert at the tail of the list *)
   VAR p: PtPrssDescr;
BEGIN IF list = NIL THEN list: = toInsert;
   ELSE p: = list;
      WHILE p↑.next # NIL DO p: = p↑.next END;
      p↑.next: = toInsert;
   END;
   toInsert↑.next: = NIL
END InsertTail;

PROCEDURE NextPriority (VAR priority:TPriority);
(* starting at 'priority', finds the highest priority non-empty ready list;
   the existence of the Idle process guarantees that there will always be
   one *)
BEGIN
   WHILE Ready[priority] = NIL DO priority: = priority – 1;
   END;
END NextPriority;

PROCEDURE P (VAR s: Semaphore);
   VAR blocked: PtPrssDescr;
BEGIN s↑.n: = s↑.n – 1;
   IF s↑.n < 0 THEN (* block the process *)
      RemoveHead (Ready[CurrentPriority], blocked);
      InsertTail (s↑.waiting, blocked); (* queue the process on tail of the
         semaphore's list *)
      NextPriority (CurrentPriority); (* finds the next CurrentPriority *)
      TRANSFER (blocked↑.prss, Ready[CurrentPriority]↑.prss)
         (* the process at the head of list Ready[CurrentPriority] becomes
            active *)
   END;
END P;

PROCEDURE V (VAR s: Semaphore);
   VAR awakened, suspended: PtDescrPrss;
      priority: TPriority; (* priority of the awakened process *)
```

```
BEGIN s↑.n: = s↑.n + 1
  IF s↑.n ≤ 0 THEN (* at least one process waiting *)
    RemoveHead (s↑.waiting, awakened);
      (* removes the process at the head of the semaphore's list *)
    priority: = awakened↑.priority;
    InsertTail (Ready[priority], awakened);
    IF priority > CurrentPriority THEN (* the awakened process will become
                                          active *)
      suspended: = Ready[CurrentPriority]; (* the currently active process is
                                              suspended *)
      CurrentPriority: = priority;
      TRANSFER (suspended↑.prss, Ready[CurrentPriority]↑.prss);
        (* the awakened process becomes active *)
    END;
  END;
END V;

PROCEDURE InitSemaphore (VAR s: Semaphore; n: INTEGER);
BEGIN NEW(s);
  s↑.n: = n; s↑.waiting: = NIL;
END InitSemaphore;

PROCEDURE WaitInterr (vector: CARDINAL);
(* suspends the calling process, waiting for an interrupt, using the vector
  given as parameter *)
  VAR waitingInterr: PtPrssDescr;
    p: PROCESS;
    priority: TPriority; (* priority of process waiting for the interrupt *)
BEGIN RemoveHead (Ready[CurrentPriority], waitingInterr);
    (* the process will wait for the interrupt *)
  NextPriority (CurrentPriority);
    (* determines the new CurrentPriority *)
  p: = Ready[CurrentPriority]↑.prss;
    (* p: active process after IOTRANSFER *)
  IOTRANSFER (waitingInterr↑.prss, p, vector);
  Ready[CurrentPriority]↑.prss: = p;
    (* p: process suspended by the interrupt *)
  priority: = waitingInterr↑.priority;
  InsertHead (Ready[priority], waitingInterr);
    (* the process reactivated by the interrupt is reinserted in the list
      Ready[priority] *)
  IF priority ≥ CurrentPriority THEN (* the reactivated process continues to
                                        execute *)
```

121

```
                CurrentPriority: = priority
          ELSE (* resume execution of the process suspended by the interrupt *)
             TRANSFER (Ready[priority]↑.prss, Ready[CurrentPriority↑.prss);
          END
       END WaitInterr;


       PROCEDURE CreateProcess (P: PROC; StackSize: CARDINAL; priority:
                                INTEGER);
          (* creates a process that executes the procedure P; the second
             parameter gives the size of the stack needed, the third the
             priority of the process *)
          VAR
             created: PtPrssDescr;
             a: ADDRESS;
       BEGIN
          NEW (created); (* allocates memory for the process descriptor *)
          ALLOCATE (a, StackSize); (* allocates memory for the process stack *)
          NEWPROCESS (P, a, StackSize, created↑.prss);
          IF NOT IdleCreation THEN (* test priority *)
             IF priority < MinPriority THEN priority: = MinPriority
             ELSIF priority > MaxPriority THEN priority: = MaxPriority;
             END;
          END;
          created↑.priority: = priority;
          InsertTail (Ready[priority], created);
       END CreateProcess;


       PROCEDURE Idle; (* code of process Idle, of priority MinPriority-1 *)
       BEGIN
          LOOP
             LISTEN (* lowers the processor priority to a level at which all interrupts
                      are allowed *)
          END;
       END Idle;


       PROCEDURE EngageClockandStart (p: PROCESS);
       (* engages the clock and initiates execution of process p; at each clock
          interrupt this procedure brings about a process switch between processes
          of minimum priority *)
          CONST
             ClockVector = 100B; (* clock interrupt vector *)
             interr     ↑ = 6; (* bit no of device register used to enable clock
                                 interrupts *)
```

```
VAR
    suspended: PtPrssDescr;
    clock: PROCESS;
    ClockReg[177546B]: BITSET; (* clock status register *)
BEGIN
    INCL (ClockReg, interr); (* enables clock interrupts *)
    LOOP IOTRANSFER (clock, p, ClockVector);
        (* p becomes active; at the instant of the interrupt p designates the
            interrupted process *)
        IF CurrentPriority = MinPriority THEN
        (* interrupted process has minimum priority, so a
            process switch is performed *)
            RemoveHead (Ready[MinPriority], suspended);
            suspended↑.prss: = p;
            InsertTail (Ready[MinPriority], suspended);
            p: = Ready[MinPriority]↑.prss
            (* IOTRANSFER will cause execution of p *)
        END;
    END;
END EngageClockandStart;


PROCEDURE StartSystem;
(* called after all processes have been created; initiates execution of the
    first process *)
    VAR first: PROCESS;
BEGIN
    CurrentPriority: = MaxPriority;
    NextPriority (CurrentPriority);
        (* determines the highest priority level used *)
    first: = Ready[CurrentPriority]↑.prss;
    EngageClockandStart (first);
END StartSystem;


BEGIN (* initialization *)
    FOR i: = MinPriority–1 TO MaxPriority DO
        Ready[i]: = NIL
    END;
    IdleCreation: = TRUE;
    CreateProcess (Idle, 128, MinPriority–1); (* creates process Idle *)
    IdleCreation: = FALSE;
END SemaphoreKernel2.
```

Figure 7.15   Implementation part of SemaphoreKernel2

123

```
DEFINITION MODULE Screen;
EXPORT QUALIFIED Write;

  PROCEDURE Write (c: CHAR);
  (* writes character c on the screen *)
END Screen.


IMPLEMENTATION MODULE Screen[4];
FROM SemaphoreKernel2 IMPORT WaitInterr;

  CONST ready = 7; (* 'ready' bit of screen status register *)
        interr = 6; (* interrupt bit ... *)
        interrVector = 64B; (* address of screen interrupt vector *)

  VAR   ScreenSR [177564B]: BITSET; (* screen status register *)
        ScreenDR [177566B]: CHAR; (* screen data register *)

  PROCEDURE Write (c: CHAR); (* writes character c on the screen *)
  BEGIN
    IF NOT (ready IN ScreenSR) THEN (* device not ready *)
      INCL(ScreenSR, interr); (* set interrupt bit *)
      WaitInterr (interrVector);
      EXCL (ScreenSR, interr); (* clear interrupt bit *)
    END;
    ScreenDR: = c; (* writes character c on the screen *)
  END Write;

END Screen.
```

Figure 7.16   Example of use of procedure WaitInterr (see Figure 6.5)

7.6   EXERCISES

7.6.1 Add a procedure DestroyProcess to the kernels given in §7.3 and §7.5 that will enable a process to delete itself. Use procedure DISPOSE to free the memory space allocated to the process descriptor, and DEALLOCATE (exported from Storage) to free that used by the stack. The parameters of DEALLOCATE are the same as those of ALLOCATE.
Warning: procedure DestroyProcess will use the stack.

7.6.2 Write a kernel to implement the mailbox of §5.6. The kernel should export, among others, the two procedures Mail (box, message) and Receive box, message).

7.6.3 Write a kernel to implement the rendezvous of §5.7. The kernel should export, among others, the procedures Send(recipient, message) and Receive(sender, message). Procedure Receive should allow the rendezvous with any sender. The parameter sender should enable the process with which the rendezvous has taken place to be identified.

Chapter 8

ADA AND RENDEZVOUS

The Ada programming language, like Portal, is based on a pseudo-parallel execution scheme. Processes, called *tasks* in Ada, can be created and destroyed dynamically, and synchronization is expressed by means of the concept of the *rendezvous*, proposed initially in the CSP language [Hoare 78] (see §5.7). The rendezvous is a synchronization tool of a higher level than the monitor; consequently various syntactic constructions have to be added to the rendezvous itself to ease the solution of the different kinds of synchronization problem that can arise.

8.1   TASKS AND THE RENDEZVOUS CONCEPT

Processes in Ada are called tasks. The lifetime of a task – that is, the period during which it exists – differs between Ada and Portal. In Portal a process can be declared only in a module or in a monitor, and not in a procedure – that is, in a syntactic unit whose lifetime is that of the entire program. The Portal processes exist consequently during the whole program with the sole exception that a process terminates if it reaches the final **end** of its code. The Ada rules that regulate task lifetimes are more complex. To illustrate them consider first the simplest possible case, that of a task T declared in a procedure p:

- T is created when p is entered, so that at this instant T and the task that executes the procedure p are executed 'simultaneously';
- execution of p cannot be completed before T is finished; this means that p may become suspended, waiting for T to finish.

However, there are always possibilities for bending this rule:

- procedure p may use the instruction **abort** to force the termination of T;
- task T may express that it will terminate as soon as p reaches the final **end** of its code.

Consider now tasks as such. The following is an example of the declaration of a task (the reason for line 1 will appear in the next example):

126

```
1   task T;


2   task body T is
3   begin
4       ...
5       printer.allocate;
6       write on printer;
7       printer.release;
8       ...
9   end T;
```

Here task T uses a printer that may be claimed by other tasks: the problem is how to deal, in Ada, with the sharing of the printer among the tasks. In Portal, as we have seen, this is done by declaring a monitor that exports the procedures allocate and release. The monitor concept does not exist in Ada, but the task T can be written as though printer were a monitor: in fact, allocate and release are entries of a task printer whose role is to serialize the calls to allocate and release, which it does by means of the rendezvous.

```
task printer is
    entry allocate;                     }  specification of the task
    entry release;
end printer;


task body printer is
begin
    loop
        accept allocate;                }  body of the task
        accept release;
    end loop;
end printer;
```

We see here that a task declaration consists of two parts – a specification and a body – analogous to the definition and implementation parts respectively of a Modula-2 module; the task T in the first example has an empty specification.

Synchronization between tasks T and printer is achieved as follows. Each task executes independently of all others until

- either task T calls an entry of the task printer
- or printer executes an instruction accept.

Both a call to an entry and the execution of the instruction **accept** constitute requests for a rendezvous, and a task that makes such a request has to wait. The rendezvous takes place when the two partners – that is, the two tasks involved – arrive at the rendezvous point. Several tasks may call the same entry simultaneously, in which case the rendezvous requests are queued, with a separate queue for each entry. For the body of the task printer the successive rendezvous will occur in the order allocate, release, allocate, release, etc. The printer will be used by one processor at a time, so the sharing has been done correctly.

The task printer here uses a simplified form of the instruction **accept**. The complete syntax of this is as follows (parameters can be given, declared in parentheses as in a procedure heading):

```
accept entry_name( ... ) do
    ...
end entry_name;
```

The rendezvous between the two tasks lasts from the **do** to the **end** entry_name, the intervening statements being executed by the task that contains the **accept**. When the rendezvous is completed the partners resume independent execution; this is illustrated in Figure 8.1.

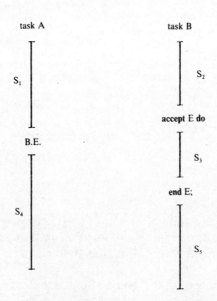

Figure 8.1   Rendezvous: statements S_1 and S_2 are executed independently by A and B respectively until B accepts entry E; B then executes S_3 until end E is reached, after which A and B execute S_4 and S_5 independently

8.2   NON-DETERMINISM: THE **SELECT** STATEMENT

As we have shown, the problem of shared use of a single printer can be solved by means of the rendezvous in the form so far described, but this form will not suffice for more complex problems. Consider the problem of sharing a variable v among a number of processes that may either read or modify it. These operations must be done in mutual exclusion. A Portal solution would declare a monitor exporting the procedures:

- **procedure** read (**var** val: integer);

- **procedure** modify (increment: integer);

Correspondingly, in Ada we should declare a task having two entries:

```
task variable_v is
   entry read (val: out integer);
   entry modify (increment: in integer);
end variable_v;
```

The reserved words **in** and **out** define the parameter passing mode: **in** means an input to the procedure (and is the default mode), **out** indicates a result given by the procedure.

We now have to write the body for this task, but we do not know in advance the order in which the entries will be called. We can express this *non-determinism* by means of the **select** statement as follows:

```
task body variable_v is
   v: integer; -- declaration of a variable[1]
begin
   v: = 0;
   loop
      select
         accept read (val: out integer) do
            val: = v;
         end read;
      or
         accept modify (increment: in integer) do
            v: = v + increment;
         end modify;
      end select;
   end loop;
end variable_v;
```

[1] -- denotes the beginning of a comment ending on the same line.

The select statement enables the task variable_v to accept a request for a rendezvous when either entry read or entry modify is called, granting the corresponding rendezvous in each case.

If we wish to initialize the variable v from outside the task variable_v we must add a third entry; this initialization must of course be done before any call of read or modify is made. Giving this new entry the name initialize, the task is now as follows:

```
task variable_v is
    entry initialize (val: in integer);
    entry read (val: out integer);
    entry modify (increment: in integer);
end variable_v;

task body variable_v is
    v: integer;
begin
    accept initialize (val: in integer) do
        v: = val;
    end initialize;
    loop
        select
            accept read (val: out integer) do
                val: = v;
            end read;
        or
            accept modify (increment: in integer) do
                v: = v + increment;
            end modify;
        end select;
    end loop;
end variable_v;
```

The first possible rendezvous is initialize and only after this has taken place can read or modify be accepted.

Finally, here is an example of a task that calls the entries of variable_v:

```
task T;

task body T is
    x, y: integer;
```

begin
  variable_v.initialize(x);
  ...
  variable_v.read(y);
  ...
end T;

8.3 SELECT STATEMENT WITH GUARDS: APPLICATION TO THE PRODUCER/CONSUMER PROBLEM

We introduced the producer/consumer problem in §5.5. It would be solved in Portal by means of a monitor buffer that exported procedures deposit and remove; in Ada we should use a task buffer with entries deposit and remove:

```
task buffer is
    entry deposit (mess: in message);
    entry remove (mess: out message);
end buffer;
```

Use of **select** enables this task to express its readiness to accept either deposit or remove rendezvous at any time. This, however, is not entirely satisfactory because it may be able to accept deposit only when the buffer is not full, and remove only when it is not empty. Such a restriction is expressed by preceding the **accept** with a condition, called a *guard* and introduced by the reserved word **when**. This is shown in Figure 8.2.

```
1   task body buffer is

2   -- const
3       n: constant: = 100; -- size of buffer

4   -- var
5       buff: array (1 .. n) of message; -- buffer
6       nbr_mess: integer: = 0; -- declaration with initialization
7       inpt, outpt: integer: = 1;
8       -- indices in array buff (see Figure 5.3)

9   begin
10      loop
11        select
12        when nbr_mess < n = >
13          accept deposit (mess: in message) do
14              buff (inpt): = mess;
15          end deposit;
```

```
16          inpt: = inpt mod n + 1;
17          nbr_mess: = nbr_mess + 1;
18      or
19          when nbr_mess > 0 = >
20              accept remove (mess: out message) do
21                  mess: = buff (outpt);
22              end remove;
23          outpt: = outpt mod n + 1;
24          nbr_mess: = nbr_mess - 1;

25          end select;
26      end loop;
27  end buffer;
```

Figure 8.2   Producer/consumer problem: solution using rendezvous

The guarded **select** is implemented as follows. Every time the **select** statement is encountered *all* the guards are evaluated; rendezvous can be made only at the entries for which the guard conditions are satisfied – that is, for which the guards evaluate to true – or at unguarded entries. The entries, of either kind, that can be accepted form what are called the open branches of the **select** statement. If there is no open branch an error condition, called an exception, is raised. In Figure 8.2 we have:

- if $nbr\_mess = 0$, only the first guard is true, so only the deposit rendezvous is possible;
- if $0 < nbr\_mess < n$, both guards are true and both rendezvous are possible;
- if $nbr\_mess = n$, only the second guard is true, so only the remove rendezvous is possible.

After the rendezvous is completed the task buffer updates nbr_mess, inpt and outpt (lines 16–17 and 23–24 in Figure 8.2); it then executes **select** again, leading to a new evaluation of the guards and a new wait for a rendezvous.

8.4   VARIANTS OF THE **SELECT** STATEMENT

We now introduce some variants of the **select** statement that allow more flexibility in the expressions for requests for and acceptances of rendezvous.

8.4.1   Select with an else branch

One of the branches of a **select** statement can be prefaced with the reserved word else:

```
select
  when C1 = > accept E1 do ... end E1;
or
  accept E2 do ... end E2;
or
  when C3 => accept E3 do ... end E3;
else
  statements of else branch;
end select;
```

First, all the guards are evaluated so as to determine which are the open branches: that is, which rendezvous can be allowed. The **else** branch is executed in one or other of the following cases:

- no branch of the select statement is open;
- there is no request for an open-branch rendezvous at the time of execution of the **select** statement.

In particular, the presence of an **else** branch avoids the raising of an exception when no branch is open. In the above example the **else** branch would be executed:

- if C1 and C3 were false and E2 was not called at the time of execution of **select**;
- if C1 were false and C3 true, and neither E2 nor E3 were called at the time of execution of **select**;

and so on.

8.4.2 Select with a delay branch

One of the branches of a **select** statement can be prefaced with a delay statement:

```
select
  when C1 = > accept E1 do ... end E1;
or
  accept E2 do ... end E2;
or
  when C3 = > accept E3 do ... end E3;
or
  delay 10.0; -- delay in seconds
  statements of delay branch;
end select;
```

133

This is a variant of the **else** branch. Again, all the guards are evaluated but now if no request for an allowable rendezvous is received within the time interval stated in the **delay** statement (here 10 seconds), the statements of the delay branch are executed.

Clearly, an **else** branch is equivalent to a **delay** branch with zero delay. It follows that a **select** statement cannot have both a **delay** and an **else** branch – the **delay** branch would never be executed.

8.4.3 Select in the calling task

So far we have used the **select** statement, with its variants, only within the task that accepts the rendezvous. However, it can also be used in the task that calls an entry. Consider, for example, the entry deposit of a task buffer, and the three following requests for rendezvous:

- variant 1:   buffer.deposit (mess);
- variant 2:   **select**
                buffer.deposit (mess);
                deposited: = true;
            else
                deposited: = false;
            end select;
- variant 3:   **select**
                buffer.deposit (mess);
                deposited: = true;
            or
                delay 1.0; – – delay in seconds
                deposited: = false;
            end select;

The first variant corresponds to a normal request for a rendezvous, such as we have been using up to the present. The second is a request for an immediate rendezvous: if that cannot take place – for example, if the buffer is full – the **else** branch is executed and there is no rendezvous. The third requests a rendezvous within a maximum of one second, and if this is not granted the request is abandoned and the **delay** branch executed.

8.5 THE 'COUNT' ATTRIBUTE, WITH APPLICATION TO THE READERS/WRITERS PROBLEM

It is sometimes necessary to know the number of tasks waiting for a rendezvous. A typical case is the readers/writers problem with priority either to the readers or to the writers (see §4.6). Suppose the writers have priority; synchronization is achieved by means of a task having four entries:

```
task readers_writers is
    entry start_read;
    entry finish_read;
    entry start_write;
    entry finish_write;
end readers_writers;
```

Giving priority to the writers is equivalent to accepting the rendezvous start_read only when there is no request for a start_write rendezvous. Use of the attribute count in the expression start_write'count enables the number of tasks waiting for the rendezvous start_write to be found. If the numbers of reading and writing operations in progress are given by the variables nbr_readers and nbr_writers respectively, the conditions under which the rendezvous can be accepted are as follows:

- a reading operation can be started if start_write'count + nbr_writers = 0 – that is, if no writing is either occurring or requested;
- a writing can be started if nbr_readers + nbr_writers = 0 – that is, if neither reading nor writing is occurring;
- finish_read or finish_write is possible at any time.

With this, the task body for ensuring synchronization of readers and writers is as follows:

```
task body readers_writers is
    nbr_readers: integer: = 0; -- number of read operations in progress
    nbr_writers: integer: = 0; -- number of write operations in progress
begin
    loop
        select
            when start_write'count + nbr_writers = 0 = >
                accept start_read;
                nbr_readers: = nbr_readers + 1;
        or
            when nbr_readers + nbr_writers = 0 = >
                accept start_write;
                nbr_writers: = nbr_writers + 1;
        or
            accept finish_read;
            nbr_readers: = nbr_readers - 1;
```

```
    or
        accept finish_write;
        nbr_writers: = nbr_writers - 1;
    end select;
  end loop;
end readers_writers;
```

Figure 8.3 **Readers/writers problem, with writers priority: solution using rendezvous**

8.6 FAMILY OF ENTRIES, WITH APPLICATION TO A RESOURCE ALLOCATION PROBLEM

In §8.1 we dealt with the problem of sharing a single printer among a number of processes. We will now complicate this slightly by assuming that we have m printers available and that each task can request up to n (Exercise 4.7.4 was for the case n = 2). This can be solved by means of a task printer with entries allocate and release respectively. The latter presents no problems; it can be declared:

```
entry release (nb_printers: in number; printers_no: in printers_array);
```

where

```
subtype number is integer range 1 .. n; -- integer interval
type printers_array is array (number) of integer range 1 .. m;
```

The parameter nbr_printers tells how many printers are released; printers_no is an array containing the numbers of these released printers.

The entry allocate cannot be constructed in this way, for this rendezvous cannot be accepted unless the number of free printers is at least equal to the number requested. This would easily be expressed if Ada would allow the use of parameters of an entry in a **when** clause. Unfortunately this is not the case. A first attempt at the solution is to declare a separate entry for each number of printers requested, in this case n entries altogether:

```
task printers is
    entry allocate1 (printers_no: out printers_array);
    entry allocate2 (printers_no: out printers_array);
    ...
    entry allocaten (printers_no: out printers_array);
    entry release (nbr_printers: in number; printers_no: in printers_array);
end printers;
```

The parameter printers_no is an array giving the numbers of the printers allocated or released.

This leads to the idea of a family of entries, to enable this type of declaration to be expressed more concisely:

```
task printers is
    entry allocate(number) (printers_no: out printers_array);
    entry release(nbr_printers: in number; printers_no: in printers_array);
end printers;
```

The family of entries allocate is parametrized by the type number, declared above; there is one entry for each value defined by the type.

Figure 8.4 gives the body of the task for the case n = 2 (see definition of the sub-type number); this does not, however, show the full advantage of using the concept of family of entries. Figure 8.5, which is genuinely parametrized and valid for any value of n, shows this more clearly.

```
task body printers is
    nbr_printers_free: integer: = m; -- number of printers available for use
    busy: array (1 .. m) of boolean: = (1 .. m = > false);
        -- gives the state of each printer (declaration with
        -- initialization of the array)

    procedure allocate_a_printer (no: out number) is
    -- enables a printer to be allocated
    begin
        i: = 1;
        while busy(i) loop
            i: = i + 1;
        end loop;
        busy(i): = true;
        no: = i; -- identifies printer allocated
        nbr_printers_free: = nbr_printers_free – 1;
    end allocate_a_printer;

    procedure release_a_printer (no: in number) is
    -- enables a printer to be released
    begin
        busy (no): = false;
        nbr_printers_free: = nbr_printers_free + 1;
    end release_a_printer;
```

137

```
begin -- task body
  loop
    select
      when nbr_printers_free > = 2 = >
        accept allocate(2) (printers_no: out printers_array) do
          allocate_a_printer (printers_no(1));
          allocate_a_printer (printers_no(2));
        end allocate;
    or
      when nbr_printers_free > = 1 = >
        accept allocate(1) (printers_no: out printers_array) do
          allocate_a_printer (printers_no(1));
        end allocate;
    or
      accept release (nbr_printers: in number; printers_no: in
                       printers_array) do
        for i in 1 .. nbr_printers loop
          release_a_printer (printers_no(i));
        end loop;
      end release;

    end select;
  end loop;
end printers;
```

Figure 8.4   **Printer allocation problem: management of m printers**

```
1   task body printers is

2     nbr_printers_free: integer: = m;
3     busy: array (1 .. m) of boolean: = (1 .. m = > false);

4     procedure allocate_a_printer (no: out number) is -- see Figure 8.4
5     end allocate_a_printer;

6     procedure release_a_printer (no: in number) is -- see Figure 8.4
7     end release_a_printer;

8     begin
9       loop
10        for i in 1 .. n loop
11          -- accept rendezvous allocate(i) and release
```

138

```
12          select

13             when nbr_printers_free > = i = >
14                accept allocate(i) (printers_no: out printers_array) do
15                   for j in 1 .. i loop
16                       allocate_a_printer (printers_no(j));
17                   end loop;
18                end allocate;
19             or
20                accept release (nbr_printers: in number;
21                                 printers_no: in printers_array) do
22                   for j in 1 .. nbr_printers loop
23                      release_a_printer (printers_no(j));
24                   end loop;
25                end release;
26             else
27                null; -- empty statement

28             end select;
29          end loop; -- for i
30       end loop;
31    end printers;
```

Figure 8.5   Printer allocation problem, with m printers: use of family of entries

In this program, at each passage through the loop from Line 12 to Line 28 the task might accept

– either the rendezvous allocate(i), if i printers are free at the time,
– or the rendezvous release.

However, the branch **else** ensures that the task is not made to wait if the rendezvous cannot be granted. The solution is still not entirely satisfactory because for most of the time the task is being executed to no purpose, which is not an acceptable situation. The solution of Figure 8.5 can be improved by introducing an entry announcing a call to allocate, to be called before the entry allocate itself is called:

```
task T;

task body T is
   nbr: integer;
   printers_no: printers_array;
```

```
begin
   ...
   printers.announce_request (nbr);
   printers.allocate (nbr) (printers_no);
   ...
   printers.release (nbr, printers_no);
   ...
end T;
```

The final version is given in Figure 8.6. The loop, which constitutes the body of the task, can be separated into two parts:
- a first part (Lines 20–31) that accepts either the rendezvous announce_request or release;
- a second part (Lines 32–41) that accepts the rendezvous allocate(1) to allocate(n).

No progress can be made in the absence of requests for allocating or releasing printers, and it is the role of the first part of the task to cause a wait for one or other of these events.

```
1    task printers is
2       entry announce_request (nbr_printers: in number);
3          -- must precede any call to allocate
4       entry allocate (number) (printers_no: out printers_array);
5       entry release (nbr_printers: in number; printers_no: in printers_array);
6    end printers;


7    task body printers is

8       nbr_printers_free: integer := m;
9       busy: array (1..m) of boolean := (1..m => false);
10      requests: array (1..n) of integer := (1..n => 0);
11         -- requests(i) = number of requests for allocate(i)

12      procedure allocate_a_printer (no: out number) is
13         -- see Figure 8.4
14      end allocate_a_printer;

15      procedure release_a_printer (no: in number) is
16         -- see Figure 8.4
17      end release_a_printer;
```

```
18    begin
19      loop

20        select
21          accept announce_request (nbr_printers: in number) do
22            requests (nbr_printers) := requests (nbr_printers) + 1;
23          end announce_request;
24        or
25          accept release (nbr_printers: in number; printers_no: in
                          printers_array)
26          do
27            for i in 1 .. nbr_printers loop
28              release_a_printer (printers_no(i));
29            end loop;
30          end release;
31        end select;

32        for i in 1 .. n loop
33          while (requests(i) > 0) and (nbr_printers_free > i) loop
34            accept allocate(i) (printers_no: out printers_array) do
35              for j in 1 .. i loop
36                allocate_a_printer (printers_no(j));
37              end loop;
38            end allocate;
39            requests(i) := requests(i) - 1;
40          end loop;
41        end loop; -- for i

42      end loop;
43    end printers;
```

Figure 8.6   Final solution to the printer allocation problem

8.7 INPUT/OUTPUT PROGRAMMING AND REAL-TIME ASPECTS

The Ada name for what we have called a module is a package, and the language provides pre-defined packages for input and output. At the same time, input and output can be programmed in the Ada language itself, which provides possibilities for handling interrupts and for accessing device registers. Thus access to the screen interface we have discussed previously is expressed:

```
screen_dr: character; -- screen data register
for screen_dr use at 8#177566#;
```

Here the first line is a declaration of a variable which in the second line is linked to a hardware address, given to base 8: the syntax is base#number#.

In Ada an interrupt is treated as a call to an entry of a task; the entry is linked to an interrupt vector in the same way as a variable is linked to a hardware address:

```
task screen is
    entry screen_interr;
    for screen_interr use at 8#64#; -- address of interrupt vector
end screen;

task body screen is
    ...
begin
    ...
    accept screen_interr;
    ...
end screen;
```

The precise effect of the interrupt depends on the implementation, which could be either as

```
screen.screen_interr;
```

or as

```
select
    screen.screen.interr;
else
    null;
end select;
```

The first form corresponds to memorizing an interrupt, the second to an interrupt that is lost if not handled immediately.

To program inputs and outputs, we still need to be able to manipulate the bits of device registers; since Ada does not define a set type some other solution must be found. One possibility is to use an array of booleans, as follows:

```
type state is array (0..15) of boolean;
for state'size use 16;
    --type state is represented by 16 bits (= 1 word in PDP-11)

screen_sr: state; --screen status register
for screen_sr use at 8#177564#;
```

The second line says that the type state is to be represented with 16 bits; hence each element of the array screen_sr corresponds to one bit of the screen status register (located at octal address 177564).

Figure 8.7 gives a fully worked out example; it is a general purpose task for writing a character to a screen in interrupt mode.

```
task screen is
    entry write (c: in character); --called to write a character on the screen
    entry screen_interr; --called by the interrupt
    for screen_interr use at 8#64#;
end screen;

task body screen is
    type state is array (0..15) of boolean;
    for state'size use 16;

    screen_sr: state; -- screen status register
    for screen_sr use at 8#177564#;

    interr: constant: = 6; --no of bit in register to enable interrupt mode
    ready: constant: = 7; --no of bit showing screen ready to accept a
                            --character

    screen_dr: character; -- screen data register
    for screen_dr use at 8#177566#;

    ch: character; --used as a buffer

begin
    loop
        accept write (c: in character) do
            ch: = c; --deposits character to be written
        end write;
```

143

```
      if not screen_sr (ready) then --screen interface not ready
         screen_sr (interr): = true; --sets interrupt bit
         accept screen_interr; --waits for the interrupt
         screen_sr (interr): = false; --clears interrupt bit
      end if;
      screen_dr: = ch; --writes character ch on the screen
   end loop;
end screen;
```

Figure 8.7   Writing a character on the screen in interrupt mode

We come now to the real-time aspects of Ada – that is, to those aspects in which time enters either directly or indirectly. These involve

- the **delay** statement
- the pre-defined package calendar
- the possibility of assigning priorities to tasks.

We have already met the **delay** statement (see 8.4.2) as a possible branch of a **select** statement: but it can also be used independently of select to suspend a task for a stated period (given in seconds):

```
delay 45.0;
```

In fact, this must be taken as a minimum delay, for there is no guarantee that the task will be given the processor immediately after the delay period has expired.

The library package calendar exports, in particular, the function clock; this returns as a result the current time, given by the year, month, day and number of seconds (and fractions of a second) since the previous midnight. The statement

```
delay t - calendar.clock;
```

enables the blocking of the calling task until clock time t (at the earliest). The following code will cause an action to be executed for the first time at clock time t and then at regular intervals determined by a constant period:

```
delay t - calendar.clock;
loop
   periodic action;
   t: = t + period;
   delay t - calendar.clock;
end loop;
```

As in Portal, allocation of the processor can be influenced by giving the tasks different priorities; these are shown by a number in the specification of a task, the greater the number the higher the priority:

```
task T is
  pragma priority (4);
  entry ...;
  ...
end T;
```

However, unlike Portal, Ada has no default priority value.

8.8   COMPARISONS BETWEEN RENDEZVOUS AND MONITORS

We are going to compare the concepts of rendezvous in Ada and monitor in Portal from the points of view of:

- power of expression
- efficiency of implementation.

For the first, it is undeniable that the rendezvous is a higher level synchronization tool than the monitor. Because of this it has to be accompanied by a number of syntactic constructs in order to provide the degree of flexibility desired, thus:

- the **select** statement
- the guarded **select** statement
- the **select** statement with branches **else, delay**
- the attribute count.

Use of the rendezvous often gives a very attractive form for the expression of synchronization. This is made very clear in the solution for the readers/ writers problem, the expression in Figure 8.3 being very natural – that is, very close to the original statement of the problem.

However, a first approach to concurrent programming in Ada may generate certain feelings of unease, arising from the fact that a task is made to play two distinct roles:

- that of the task as such
- that of a mechanism for synchronization.

One of the difficulties of concurrent programming lies in the splitting of the

145

program into tasks. It is generally true that the inexperienced programmer in this field tends to introduce more tasks than are necessary – a tendency that might be accentuated by the double role of the Ada task.

Consider now the question of relative efficiencies of implementation. With monitors, synchronization involves a *passive* object, the monitor: a procedure in a monitor *is executed* by a process. In contrast, the rendezvous involves an *active* object, the task. The difference is significant from the point of view of implementation. We can illustrate this with the producer/consumer problem. Suppose a consumer wishes to take a message from the buffer at a time when the latter is neither full nor empty:

- in Portal it will call a procedure get of the monitor buffer. If the monitor is free at the moment of the call there will be no process switch and the consumer will simply take the message;
- in Ada the task consumer calls an entry get of the task buffer. The taking of the message thus involves two process switches – the first on acceptance of the rendezvous (consumer being suspended and buffer activated), the second on completion of the rendezvous (to allow consumer to resume execution).

The situation is different if the consumer asks to take a message at a moment when either the buffer is empty or the producer is blocked, waiting to deposit a message, the buffer being full. It is different also when there are several producers or consumers. We shall not go into the details of these cases; we can say, however, that a study of the question has shown that the monitor solution is the more efficient when these conditions hold:

- there are few conflicts for access to the monitor – a process will usually find that it is free;
- the buffer is never full and never empty.

The rendezvous solution is the more efficient when precisely the opposites of these conditions hold [Eventoff 80].

8.9 EXERCISES

8.9.1 Solve the printer allocation problem with n printers, and each task allowed to request only a single printer.

8.9.2 Solve the producer/consumer problem for the case in which the buffer capacity is only one message and the producer puts its messages there without checking to see if the previous message has been used (see §5.8.5).

8.9.3 Solve Exercise 6.6.2 (management of two resources) using rendezvous.

8.9.4 Show how semaphores can be implemented in Ada.

8.9.5 Solve the readers/writers problem with priority to the readers.

8.9.6 Solve the same problem with equal priorities.

Chapter 9

AN EXAMPLE OF DESIGNING A CONCURRENT PROGRAM

Based on one example, this chapter shows how one goes about designing a concurrent program; the general approach is that of a paper by Gomaa [Gomaa 84]. The solution to the problem of the example is given in each of the three languages Portal, Modula-2 and Ada, thus extending Chapters 6, 7 and 8 respectively by a complete program.

9.1 STATEMENT OF THE PROBLEM

The criteria for the choice of problem were that it should not be so difficult as to preclude a complete treatment and not so simple that the solution was obvious. The problem chosen was the implementation of a digital clock and chronometer, offering the following services:

- the clock must display the time of day on the screen at a terminal, with the format hh:mm:ss (hour, minutes, seconds respectively), eg 09:10:24;
- the chronometer must display an elapsed time on the same terminal.

These displays are provided in response to certain commands typed on the keyboard. For the clock:

- the command S (stop) stops the clock;
- after the clock has been stopped, the time displayed is set by typing h, m, s: h increments the hour by one unit, modulo 24; m the minutes modulo 60, without any carry-over to h; and s the seconds modulo 60 without carry-over to m;
- R (restart) restarts the clock.

At the start of the program the clock display is set to 00:00:00.
The chronometer, like the clock, can be either stopped or running. When stopped it shows 00:00:00; it responds to these commands:

- C (chronometer) starts the chronometer;
- after it has been started the command I (intermediate) causes the elapsed time since starting to be displayed, with a precision of 1/100 of a second. This display lasts for three seconds, after which the counting

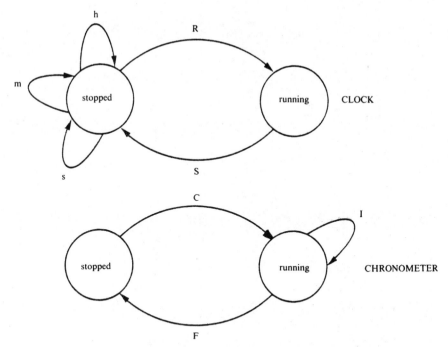

Figure 9.1   State transitions for clock and chronometer

of the time continues, catching up the time elapsed during the display;
- the command F (final) displays the final time, again to 1/100 seconds. This display lasts for five seconds, after which it resets to the initial 00:00:00 ready for the next time measurement.

Thus both the clock and the chronometer can be in either of two states:

- stopped
- running (or working).

Figure 9.1 shows the state transition diagram for the clock and for the chronometer; the initial state of both is stopped.

9.2   DATA FLOW ANALYSIS

A good way to start thinking about a problem is to analyse the data flow, for this will make clear what processes must be provided in the program: the choice of processes presents one of the main difficulties in designing a concurrent program.

The data flow for the clock/chronometer problem is shown in Figure 9.2;

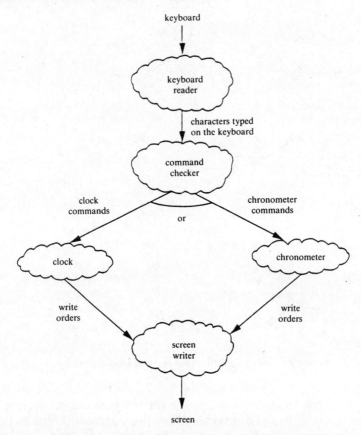

Figure 9.2 Data flow for the clock/chronometer problem

here the arcs represents the data flowing through the system and the balloons the transformations applied. A data transformer accepts input data and produces an output – which can be the same as the input. The figure shows five transformers:

- the keyboard reader, that outputs the characters read from the keyboard;
- the command checker, that analyses the commands entered and passes on those that are legal: for the clock R, S, h, m, s and for the chronometer C, I, F (see Figure 9.1);
- the clock, that receives R, S, h, m, s as input, and outputs instructions for writing on the screen. These write orders cause the time displayed to change, with a write order every second; in the absence of write orders the display remains constant;
- the chronometer, that receives C, I, F as input and like the clock outputs orders for writing on the screen, showing the passage of time as measured by the chronometer;

- the screen writer, that receives the characters to be written and writes them on the screen.

From these we can see at once how to deal with the recording of the intermediate time: no other write order must be sent to the screen during the three seconds for which this display lasts, and the first write order after that must take into account the elapsed time. The same principle can be applied to the five seconds of the display of the chronometer's final time.

9.3   BREAKDOWN INTO PROCESSES

Starting from the dataflow analysis we can now attempt to identify the elements that will form the processes. Gomaa has given six criteria for deciding when to implement a data transformer as a process [Gomaa 84]:

- input/output dependence. A transformer that either receives its input from a peripheral or sends its output to a peripheral must run at a speed determined by the peripheral. It must therefore be made into a process;
- time-critical function. If there are real-time constraints on the transformation then this must be performed by a process, so that it can be given high priority;
- computationally intensive function. If the transformation involves heavy computation and is not time-critical it should be done by a process so that it can be given low priority, and thus will not interfere with time-critical processes;
- functional cohesion. If a number of transformers interact strongly it is sensible to group these together into a single process, thus avoiding the costs of inter-process communication;
- temporal cohesion. Transformers that must act at the same instant – for example, in response to the same interrupt – should be grouped together into a single process;
- periodic execution. A transformer that is to execute at regular intervals is most naturally implemented as a process.

In our problem input/output dependence applies to reading from the keyboard and writing on the screen (see Figure 9.2); so for a start we have two processes, a keyboard reader and a screen writer. Periodic execution applies to both clock and chronometer, so we have two more processes. With these four processes (see Figure 9.3) we have several instances of the producer/consumer problem:

- between the processes **read** and **clock**: transmission of commands to the clock;

151

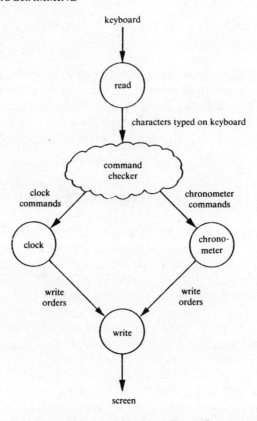

keyboard

read

characters typed on keyboard

command
checker

clock
commands

chronometer
commands

clock

chrono-
meter

write
orders

write
orders

write

screen

Figure 9.3 Clock/chronometer problem: data flow and processes (circles)

- between read and chronometer: transmission of commands to the chronometer;
- between clock and write: transmission of the time of day;
- between chronometer and write: transmission of measured elapsed time.

From here on the development of the solution depends on the primitives available for synchronization, so the details will vary according to the language used.

9.4 SOLUTION IN PORTAL

The various producer/consumer problems just mentioned are solved in Portal with the help of monitors. The structure of such a solution is given in Figure 9.4: the process read puts the characters read from the keyboard into either the monitor clock_command (for sending to the clock) or the monitor chrono_command (for sending to the chronometer). These monitors are

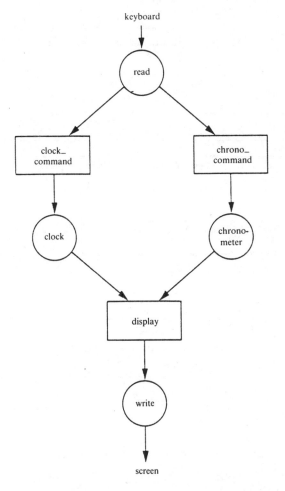

Figure 9.4   Portal solution: data flow, processes (circles) and monitors (rectangles)

responsible also for checking the commands. The processes clock and chronometer put the write orders in the monitor display, from which they are taken by the process write.

Filling in the details for this outline structure gives the final form of Figure 9.5, which we will now discuss.

Since a signal, here associated with an interrupt, can be declared only in a monitor we must add a further monitor for reading from the keyboard: call this keyboard and let it export the procedure read, thus enabling characters to be read when typed on the keyboard. We have dealt with this problem in §6.3 so we shall not consider it further here.

Figure 9.6 gives the process read that transmits each character read either to the buffer clock_command or to chrono_command.

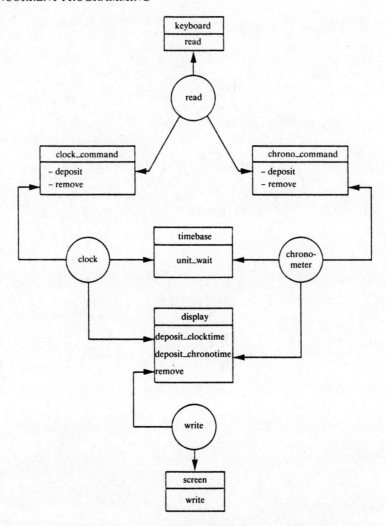

Figure 9.5   Portal solution: processes are represented by circles, monitors (with the procedures exported) by rectangles and procedure calls by arrows

The monitor clock_command has a one-character buffer, representing one command (there is no need for this buffer to be any greater). It exports the procedures deposit and remove, deposit being called by read and remove by clock. A command may change the state of the clock (see Figure 9.1) and it can be seen that the management of this state is best done inside the monitor clock_command, when a remove call is made. Actually we consider the clock state to change when the command is received by the process clock, and not

```
process read;
uses keyboard, clock_command, chrono_command; (* monitors imported *)
  var ch: char; (* command read *)
code
  loop
    keyboard.read (ch);
    case ch
      of 'S', 'R', 'h', 'm', 's': clock_command.deposit(ch);
      of 'C', 'I', 'F': chrono_command.deposit(ch);
      else (* ignore command *)
    end case
  end loop
end read;
```

Figure 9.6   Process read

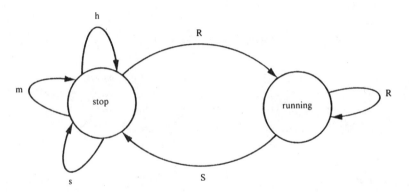

Figure 9.7   Commands seen by the process clock, after filtering by the monitor
clock_command

when it is placed in the buffer. The clock state has an effect also on the procedure remove:

- if the buffer is empty and the clock is stopped, remove must block the process clock, causing it to wait for one or other of R (restart), h (hour), m (minute), s (second);
- if the buffer is empty and the clock is running, remove must not block clock for then it would no longer keep the correct time; remove must therefore return the command R, which is simply the command last read (Figure 9.1).

How should remove treat the command S (stop)? One possibility is to block clock when the latter removes the command S, but we have adopted another:

155

S is transmitted to clock so as to enable it to reset the fractions of a second to zero – these are not displayed on the screen, but are logically zero when the clock is stopped. It is only the following call to remove that blocks clock.

Figure 9.7 shows the commands as seen by the clock, after filtering by the monitor clock_command. The monitor itself is given by Figure 9.8.

```
monitor clock_command;
defines deposit, remove;

  var clock_state: (stopped, running);
      buffer: char; (* for a command *)
      buffer_state: (empty, full);

  signal
    not_empty, not_full;

  procedure deposit (command: char);
  code
    if buffer_state = full then not_full.wait end if;

    (* deposits the command only if it is correct according to the clock
       state *)
    if (clock_state = running) = (command = 'S') then
      buffer: = command; (* deposit command *)
      buffer_state: = full; not_empty.send;
    end if;
  end deposit;

  procedure remove (var command: char);
  code
    case clock_state
    of stopped:
      if buffer_state = empty then not_empty.wait end if;
      command: = buffer;
      if command = 'R' then clock_state: = running end if;
    of running:
      (* if the buffer is empty, it still contains 'R' *)
      command: = buffer;
      if command = 'S' then clock_state: = stopped end if;
    end case;
    buffer_state: = empty; not_full.send;
  end remove;
```

```
code (* initialization *)
  clock_state: = stopped;
  buffer_state: = empty;
end clock_command;
```

Figure 9.8 Monitor clock_command

Part of the action of process clock is thus performed by the procedure remove in the monitor clock_command. This procedure provides the following commands (see Figure 9.7):

- R (restart), causing the clock to run. The process clock must allow one unit of time to elapse (typically 20 msec), increment the time and, in case one second has elapsed since the last change, update the display;
- S (stop), resetting to zero the fractions of a second in the time;
- h, m, s (hours, minutes and seconds respectively) indicating that the clock, which is stopped, must be reset. Both internal and display time must be changed.

A time will be displayed on the screen as a result of putting a string of characters into the buffer display (Figure 9.5). The monitor display exports three procedures:

- deposit_clocktime; puts in the buffer a string corresponding to the time as given by the clock;
- deposit_chronotime; puts in the buffer a string corresponding to the latest time measure given by the chronometer;
- remove, called by the process write.

The details are given in Appendix 2.

The wait of one time unit is achieved in Portal by waiting for a signal with timeout (see §6.4). Since a signal can be declared only in a monitor, this is provided by a call to a procedure unit_wait of a monitor timebase (Figure 9.9). As we have said previously, on a PDP-11, one time unit is 20 ms or 2/100 of a second.

```
monitor timebase;
defines unit_wait;
  signal s; (* must be declared in a monitor *)
  procedure unit_wait;
  (* suspends the process for 1 time unit (20 ms) *)
    var b: boolean;
```

157

```
      code
          s.wait (delay ==1, timeout =:b);
      end unit_wait;
  end timebase;
```

Figure 9.9   Monitor timebase

An important question must be raised here: how accurate is the time thus measured? The process clock can be modelled as follows:

```
  process clock;
  code
    loop
        remove a command;
        timebase.unit_wait;
        increment clocktime;
    end loop;
  end clock;
```

It might be thought that if the time taken to execute the instructions in the loop is n milliseconds, the waiting being 20 ms, the true length of time that elapses between incrementations is not 20 ms but 20 + n. But this is not so, owing to the implementation of a wait with delay given in Figure 6.8 (§6.4): a wait with delay one corresponds in reality to a wait for the next clock interrupt (these occurring every 20 ms) rather than a suspension for 20 ms. So long as the time between successive calls of unit_wait is always less than 20 ms – which is amply satisfied in our case – the time as measured will be correct. Figure 9.10 gives the process clock.

```
  process clock;
  uses clock_command, timebase, display; (* monitors imported *)
    var clocktime:...; (* time managed by the clock *)
        command: char; (* command read *)

  code
      initialize clocktime to 00:00:00;
      display.deposit_clocktime(clocktime); (* displays 00:00:00 *)
      loop
        clock_command.remove (command);
        case command

        of 'R': (* clock running *)
          timebase.unit_wait;
```

```
    increment clocktime by one unit;
    if 1 second elapsed since last display then
        display.deposit_clocktime(clocktime);
    end if;
of 'S': (* clock stopped *)
    set fractions of a second in clocktime to 0;
of 'h': (* clock stopped *)
    increment the hours field modulo 24;
    display.deposit_clocktime (clocktime);
of 'm': (* clock stopped *)
    increment the minutes field modulo 60;
    display.deposit_clocktime (clocktime);
of 's': (* clock stopped *)
    increment the seconds field modulo 60;
    display.deposit_clocktime (clocktime);

    end case;
  end loop;
end clock;
```

Figure 9.10 Process clock

The treatment of the clock will be based on that of the chronometer. We see from Figure 9.5 that for this we need to introduce

- a process chronometer
- a monitor chrono_command.

We have already seen how to deal with the display of the intermediate and final times: these remain on the screen, unchanged, for three and five seconds respectively, during which no further write instructions are sent to the screen. We must, however, tackle these questions:

- how should we deal with a command I (requesting intermediate time) or F (final time) received in a three-second period during which the intermediate time is being displayed?
- how should we treat a command C, to restart the chronometer, received in a five-second period during which the final time is being displayed?

In the first case the time requested, whether intermediate or final, will be displayed immediately; in the second, the chronometer will be restarted immediately.

Another question is whether the times for the display of intermediate and final times should be calculated in the same way; the answer is no. To make

159

the expression for the solution close to the original statement of the problem, we decide that the process chronometer shall be halted, waiting for the command C, precisely while the chronometer is in the state stopped (see Figure 9.1). Thus the process is active during the time of the display of the intermediate time and, given the monitor timebase, can therefore calculate the required three seconds. This is not possible in the case of the final time, for the process chronometer is then blocked in the monitor chrono_command, waiting for the command C. To explain how we deal with these five seconds for the display we need to consider two stopped states, as shown in Figure 9.11:

- 'final stopped', with the final elapsed time displayed;
- 'initial stopped', with the display 00:00:00.

In the final stopped state the chronometer waits either for five seconds to elapse or for the user to type in the command C. This is implemented in the monitor chrono_command by waiting for a command with a maximum delay of five seconds; the process chronometer is informed of the end of this delay by receiving a fictious command R (re-initialize the time displayed). Command R, followed immediately by C is sent also if C is typed before the expiry of the five seconds (see Figure 9.12).

The texts for the monitor chrono_command and the process chronometer are given in Figure 9.13 and 9.14 respectively. The complete solution in Portal to the problem is given in Appendix 2.

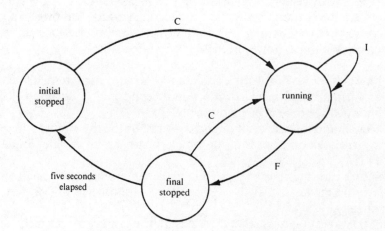

Figure 9.11   Modified state transition diagram for the chronometer

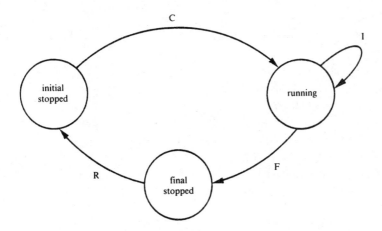

Figure 9.12 Commands seen by the process *chronometer*, after filtering by the
chrono_command

```
monitor chrono_command;
defines deposit, remove;

  const
    sec5 = 250; (* 5 seconds = 250 units of 20 msec *)

  var
    chrono_state: (initial_stopped, final_stopped, running);

    buffer: char; (* for one command *)
    buffer_state: (empty, full);

  signal
    not_empty, not_full;

procedure deposit (command: char);
code
    if buffer_state = full then not_full.wait end if;
    (* puts the command in the buffer if and only if it is correct according to
       the chronometer state, see Figure 9.1 *)
    if (chrono_state = running) ≠ (command = 'C') then
      buffer: = command;
      buffer_state: = full; not_empty.send;
    end if;
end deposit;
```

```
    procedure remove (var command: char);
      var b: boolean; (* for wait with delay *)
    code
      case chrono_state

      of initial_stopped:
        if buffer_state = empty then not_empty.wait end if;
        (* remove the command, which must be 'C' *)
          command: = buffer;
        chrono_state: = running; (* since the command was 'C' *)
        buffer_state: = empty; not_full.send;

      of running:
        (* if the buffer is empty the fictious 'C' is sent *)
        if buffer_state = empty then command: = 'C' else command: = buffer
        end if;
        if command = 'F' then chrono_state: = final_stopped end if;
        buffer_state: = empty; not_full.send;

      of final_stopped:
        if buffer_state = empty then (* wait for at most 5 seconds *)
          not_empty.wait (delay == sec5, timeout =:b)
        end if;
        (* in all cases return the fictious command 'R', without emptying the
          buffer; see Figure 9.12 *)
        command: = 'R'; chrono_state: = initial_stopped;

      end case;
    end remove;

  code (* initialization *)
    chrono_state: = initial_stopped;
    buffer_state: = empty;
  end chrono_command;
```

Figure 9.13   Monitor chrono_command

```
process chronometer;
uses chrono_command, timebase, display; (* monitors imported *)

  var
    chronotime: ...; (* time interval measured by the chronometer *)
```

AN EXAMPLE OF DESIGNING A CONCURRENT PROGRAM

```
inter_chronotime: boolean; (* true if an intermediate time is displayed *)
end_inter_chronotime: ...; (* time of end of display of an intermediate
                              time *)

command: char; (* command read *)

code
  command: = 'R'; (* initializes and displays time below *)
  loop
    case command

        of 'R': (* fictious initialization command *)
          initialize chronotime to 00:00:00;
          display.deposit_chronotime (chronotime);
          inter_chronotime: = false;

        of 'C': (* chronometer running *)
          timebase.unit_wait;
          increment chronotime by one unit;
          if inter_chronotime then (* is end of intermediate time reached? *)
            inter_chronotime: = chronotime ≠ end_inter_chronotime;
          end if;
          if one second has elapsed since the last display and not
            inter_chronotime
            then display.deposit_chronotime (chronotime)
          end if;

        of 'I': (* intermediate chronotime, chronometer running *)
          inter_chronotime: = true;
          end_inter_chronotime: = chronotime + three seconds;
          (* displays the intermediate time *)
          display.deposit_chronotime (chronotime to 1/100 secs);

        of 'F': (* final chronotime, displayed to 1/100 secs *)
          display.deposit_chronotime (chronotime to 1/100 secs);

    end case;
    chrono_command.remove (command)
  end loop;
end chronometer;
```

Figure 9.14   Process chronometer

163

9.5   SOLUTION IN MODULA-2

The first step towards a Modula-2 solution is the choice of a kernel, and at first sight there seem to be the following two possibilities:

- either implement the Portal kernel in Modula-2;
- or adapt the semaphore kernel of §7.5 by incorporating a delayed wait (for example in the form of a procedure PwithDelay).

The first has the attraction of taking over the Portal solution as it is, but the implementation of the Portal kernel in Modula-2 would be relatively lengthy. The second would require the synchronization achieved by the monitors clock_command, chrono_command and display to be translated into semaphore terms.

There is, however, a third possibility with the following advantages:

- the kernel is not too difficult to implement
- the expression of the synchronization is close to that of Portal

and this is the one we shall adopt. The basic idea is to make a partial implementation of the Portal kernel, omitting the procedures for entering and leaving the monitor (see §6.5). Mutual exclusion of access to the monitor, achieved by these procedures, must therefore be imposed by some different mechanism. The solution is to replace the monitor by a module declared with priority 7, which on the PDP-11 inhibits all interrupts. Figure 9.15 illustrates this in the case of the producer/consumer problem.

```
DEFINITION MODULE Buffer;
EXPORT QUALIFIED Deposit, Remove;

    PROCEDURE Deposit (c: CHAR);

    PROCEDURE Remove (VAR c: CHAR);

END Buffer.

IMPLEMENTATION MODULE Buffer [7]; (* priority 7 ensures mutual
                                               exclusion *)
FROM Kernel IMPORT
    (*type *) Signal,
    (* procedures *) Wait, Send, InitSignal;

    VAR notfull, notempty: Signal;
```

```
PROCEDURE Deposit (c: CHAR);
BEGIN
   IF buffer full THEN Wait (notfull) END;
   deposit c in the buffer;
   Send (notempty);
END Deposit;

PROCEDURE Remove (VAR c: CHAR);
BEGIN
   IF buffer empty THEN Wait (notempty) END;
   remove a character from the buffer;
   Send (notfull);
END Remove;

BEGIN (* initialization *)
   InitSignal (notfull);
   InitSignal (notempty);
   ...
END Buffer.
```

Figure 9.15   Modula-2 solution for the producer/consumer problem: the monitor is replaced by a module declared at priority 7

We must note that the solution given in Figure 9.15 is not strictly equivalent to the Portal monitor solution. Consider the following case, starting from the situation in which the producer process is waiting for the signal notfull:

- process consumer calls the procedure Remove and sends the signal notfull; we assume that Send, as in Portal, causes a process switch;
- process producer acquires the processor, deposits its message and leaves the module Buffer.

Here there is nothing to prevent process producer from executing Deposit afresh, whereas Portal would consider the monitor as being occupied by process consumer at this moment. However, this difference in the semantics has no consequences when the call to Send is the last instruction before leaving the monitor, as is the case in Figure 9.15 and in all the monitors of §9.4.

The kernel we shall use exports the type Signal, the procedures InitSignal (to initialize a signal), Wait, Send, WaitInterr (to wait for an interrupt), Delay (to suspend a process for a time given as a parameter) and WaitDelay (to suspend a process until either an interrupt is received or a specified delay has expired). Figure 9.16 shows the data structures employed in the implementation. The processes, whether ready or waiting, are arranged in a circular

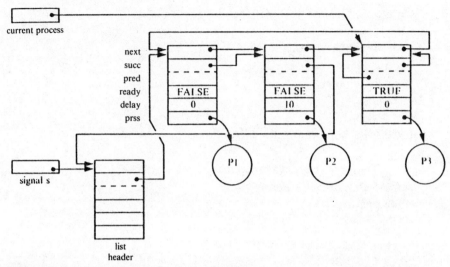

Figure 9.16 Data structures of the kernel. For the sake of clarity, not all the pointers *pred* are shown

list, an arrangement that reduces the number of operations involved in manipulating the list and is permissible because no priorities are assigned to processes. A descriptor for each process contains the following information:

- a link used to implement the circular list of all the processes;
- a double link to enable a process to be inserted into the waiting list of a signal;
- a boolean to show whether or not the process is ready: only ready processes are eligible to be given the processor;
- an integer, used in the implementation of a wait with delay. If this field contains a value different from zero the process is waiting for a delay to expire, and is therefore not ready; the delay is decremented by one unit at each clock interrupt until it reaches zero; at that moment the process becomes ready again;
- a field of type PROCESS.

In Figure 9.16 process P3 is ready, P1 is waiting for the signal s and P2 is waiting either for this signal or for a delay of 10 units to expire.

Some explanation is needed of the implementation of a list associated with a signal. The double chaining – with both forwards- and backwards-pointing links – makes it possible to remove a process from the list when a delay expires before the signal is received. The list header, shown in Figure 9.16, is of the same type as the elements of the list; it enables the operations of insertion into and removal from the list to be simplified, with no special treatment needed if the list is empty or has only a single element. Figure 9.17 shows how an empty list is represented.

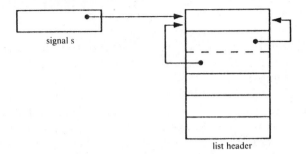

signal s

list header

Figure 9.17   Representation of the empty list

Appendix 3 gives the module that implements this kernel, and the adaptation to Modula-2 of the Portal solution of §9.5. Notice that the monitor timebase has disappeared here: the wait of a unit of time is brought about by the kernel procedure Delay.

9.6   SOLUTION IN ADA

The structure of the Ada program does not differ fundamentally from that of either the Portal (Figure 9.5) or the Modula-2 program. The monitors of the Portal solution must however disappear, and before considering their replacements we should note the different roles of the various monitors of Figure 9.5:

- clock_command, chrono_command and display implement buffers (between producer and consumer processes);
- timebase enables a process to be suspended for one unit of time: in Portal a signal, and therefore a monitor, has to be introduced in order to cause a wait;
- keyboard and screen take care of input and output: again, a wait for an interrupt requires a signal and therefore a monitor.

As we showed in §8.2, in Ada a buffer is realized by means of a task; thus clock_command, chrono_command and display are replaced by tasks, which can have the same names.

There is no replacement for timebase, suspension of a process for a specified time being expressed in Ada using the **delay** statement. To be more precise we shall use the statement

delay system.tick;

where the constant tick is declared in the predefined package system (package being the Ada name for a module). The value of system.tick, which depends on the implementation, corresponds to one cycle of the machine clock. We shall assume that for our target machine, the PDP-11, **delay** system.tick suspends a task until the next clock interrupt arrives; as we saw in §9.4, this ensures that the time is measured accurately.

An interrupt is implemented in Ada as a call to a task entry, so the Portal monitors keyboard and screen are replaced by tasks of the same names. The temporal cohesion criterion of §9.3 suggests that the tasks keyboard and read should be combined into a single task read, and screen and write into a single task write. The structure of the resulting program is given in Figure 9.18.

We shall not go into the details of all the tasks of Figure 9.18 but we must take up one particularly important point, concerning the task chrono_command which implements a buffer between read and chronometer.

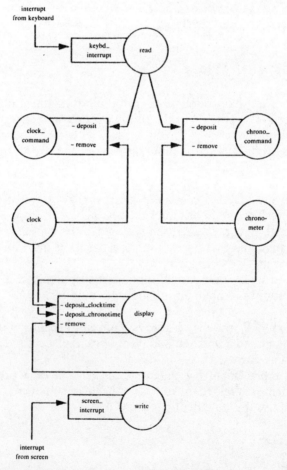

Figure 9.18   Structure of the Ada program. Circles represent tasks, rectangles, task entries and arrows calls to the entries

In the corresponding Portal monitor we have used the call to the kernel

```
not_empty.wait(delay == 5 seconds, ...);
```

to suspend the process chronometer (in the state final_stopped) either until a command is received or until a delay of five seconds has expired (Figure 9.13). To express this in Ada we use the instruction **select** with a **delay** branch:

```
when (chrono_state = final_stopped) and (buffer_state = empty) =>
    delay 5.0; -- 5 seconds delay
```

This can be seen in the program text of Figure 9.19. If the chronometer is in the state final_stopped and the buffer is empty only two of the guards of the select statement are open, those of the branches deposit and **delay**. Thus the delay branch, which provides the fictious R command, is executed when the following conditions hold:

- the chronometer is in the state final_stopped and the buffer is empty;
- the entry deposit has not been called before the five seconds delay has expired.

```
task chrono_command is
-- implements a buffer between read and chronometer
    entry deposit (command: character);
    entry remove (command: out character);
end chrono_command;


task body chrono_command is

-- type
    type t_chrono_state is (initial_stopped, running, final_stopped);
    type t_buffer_state is (empty, full);

-- var
    chrono_state: t_chrono_state;

    buffer: character; --buffer for one command
    buffer_state: t_buffer_state;

begin
    chrono_state: = initial_stopped; buffer_state: = empty;
    loop
```

169

```
    select

        when buffer_state = empty =>
            accept deposit (command: character) do
                -- put only a legal command in the buffer
                if (chrono_state = running) ≠ (command = 'C') then
                    buffer: = command; buffer_state: = full;
                end if;
            end deposit;
    or
        when (chrono_state = initial_stopped) and (buffer_state = full) =>
            accept remove (command: out character) do
                --command must be 'C'
                command: = buffer;
            end remove;
            chrono_state: = running;
            buffer_state: = empty;
    or
        when chrono_state = running =>
            accept remove (command: out character) do
                -- provides 'C' if buffer is empty
                if buffer_state = empty then buffer: = 'C'; end if;
                command: = buffer;
            end remove;
            if buffer = 'F' then chrono_state: = final_stopped; end if;
            buffer_state: = empty;
    or
        when (chrono_state = final_stopped) and (buffer_state = full) =>
            accept remove (command: out character) do
                -- provides fictious 'R' without emptying the buffer
                command: = 'R';
            end remove;
            chrono_state: = initial_stopped;
    or
        when (chrono_state = final_stopped) and (buffer_state = empty) =>
            delay 5.0; -- 5 seconds
            accept remove (command: out character) do
                command: = 'R'; -- fictious 'R'
            end remove;
            chrono_state: = initial_stopped;
```

170

```
    end select;
  end loop;
end chrono_command;
```

Figure 9.19 Task chrono_command

One further point in the Ada solution is worth noting, concerning the tasks read and write. One's first idea when trying to adapt the Portal solution might be to declare a procedure kb_read (corresponding to read of the monitor keyboard) local to the task read, and a procedure scr_write (corresponding to write of the monitor screen) local to the task write. But then the wait for the interrupt (ie the **accept** statement) would be in the procedure kb_read or scr_write, while an **accept** statement is allowed only in the body of a task. The complete Ada solution is given in Appendix 4.

9.7   CONCLUSION

While the details vary according to the language used, the solutions in Portal, Modula-2 and Ada respectively do not differ greatly. Much of the difficulty of constructing a concurrent program lies in the design of the structure and the choice of processes. To a large extent this is independent of the language. Very roughly, the amount of effort needed is divided in the following way:

- 2/3 in designing the structure of the program (practically independent of the language);
- 1/3 in writing the actual program (dependent on the language).

9.8   EXERCISES

9.8.1 Add a chime to the clock of the problem treated in this chapter. It is to strike the hour – one stroke for one o'clock, two strokes for two o'clock, etc; a command to stop the clock must not stop a chime that has already started. (Use the character bell, ASCII code 7).

9.8.2 Add an alarm, to sound at a time specified by the user; it is to be stopped by striking a single key on the keyboard.

9.8.3 Generalize question 9.8.2 to sound the alarm at a series of specified times and display a previously-input message on the terminal screen at each sounding.

Appendix 1

NOTATION USED FOR THE ALGORITHMS

Throughout this book, except for the chapters on Modula-2 and Ada, we have used the syntax of the Portal language to express the algorithms: this should present no difficulty to the reader familiar with Pascal. At the same time, we have taken a few liberties with the Portal syntax in the interest of easy reading of the algorithms.

One thing that needs to be made clear is the concept of a module. A module is a programming unit that enables constants, types, variables, procedures and functions that are logically related to be grouped together. An example is the implementation of a stack: this can be achieved by means of a module, as follows:

```
1   module stack;
2   defines push, pop; (* procedures exported by the module *)

3     const
4         max = 100; (* maximum size of stack *)

5     var
6         vstack: array 1 .. max of integer;
7             (* array in which the stack will be implemented *)
8         top: 0 .. max;
9             (* pointer to the top of the stack *)

10    procedure push(i: integer);
11    (* pushes i on the stack *)
12    code
13      if top = max then 'error stack full'
14      else
15         top: = top + 1;
16         vstack[top]: = i;
17      end if;
18    end push;

19    procedure pop(var i: integer);
20    (* returns the value at the top of the stack *)
```

```
21    code
22      if top = 0 then 'error stack empty'
23      else
24         i: = vstack[top];
25         top: = top - 1;
26      end if;
27    end pop;

28   code (* initialization *)
29      top: = 0; (* stack initially empty *)
30   end stack;
```

This module stack groups together:

- the constant max
- the variables top, vstack
- the procedures push, pop.

Outside the module only the procedures push and pop, stated in the export list of Line 2, can be accessed; these are the procedures exported by the module. Thus a module can be looked on as a black box, about which all that is visible is the set of objects in the export list: all the details of the implementation are hidden inside.

The initialization code (Line 29 above) is executed before the start of the program; thus the variable top is initialized before the first call is made to push or pop.

A process that wishes to use this module must declare it in its own *import list*, indicated by the reserved word **uses**. The import of a module allows access to *all* the objects exported by that module:

```
process p;
uses stack; (* process p imports module stack *)
  var
    i, j: integer;
code
  ...
  stack.push(i);
  ...
  stack.pop(j);
  ...
end p;
```

Appendix 2

SOLUTION OF THE CLOCK/
CHRONOMETER PROBLEM IN PORTAL

We give here the complete solution in Portal to the problem described in Chapter 9. Input and output are expressed in the terms that apply to the PDP-11, and, contrary to the policy of the rest of the book, the Portal syntax has been strictly adhered to.

The program has the form of a main module clock_chronometer, composed of monitors and processes; these are given in the following order:

- monitor keyboard
- monitor clock_command
- monitor chrono_command
- process read
- module hmsc_operations
- monitor timebase
- monitor display
- process clock
- process chronometer
- monitor screen
- process write

These monitors, processes and modules are all declared within the main module clock_chronometer.

module clock_chronometer; (* solves the clock/chronometer problem *)

type
t_string_11 = **string** (11);
    (* string of 11 characters for the time in the form HH:MM:SS.CC, where
    CC gives the hundredths of a second; this would be declared in the
    module hmsc_operations if Portal allowed transparent export *)

t_dest = (dest_clock, dest_chrono);
    (* used by the process write, tells whether the destination of a string
    giving a time is the clock or the chronometer; again this would be

declared in the module hmsc_operations if Portal allowed transparent export *)

----

monitor [4] keyboard; (* manages the terminal's keyboard *)
defines read;

```
    type
        bits = (b0, b1, b2, b3, b4, b5, interr, ready, b8, b9, b10, b11, b12, b13,
                b14, b15,);
        state = set of bits;

    var
        keyboard_status at 177560B: state;
        keyboard_data at 177562B: char;

    signal
        interrupt [60B];

    procedure read (result c: char); (* reads a character from the keyboard *)
    uses var keyboard_status; uses keyboard_data, interrupt;
    code
        if ready not in keyboard_status then (* no character has been typed *)
            keyboard_status: = keyboard_status + state(interr);
            interrupt.wait; (* waits for a character *)
            keyboard_status: = keyboard_status – state(interr);
        end if;
        c: = keyboard_data; (* reads character typed *)
        if ord(c) >= 200B then (* suppress the parity bit *)
            c: = chr(ord(c) – 200B);
        end if;
    end read;

end keyboard;
```

----

monitor clock_command; (* manages a buffer between processes read and
                            clock *)
defines deposit, remove;

175

```
var
   clock_state: (stopped, running);

   buffer: char; (* for a command *)
   buffer_state: (empty, full);

signal
   not_empty, not_full;

procedure deposit (command: char);
uses var buffer, buffer_state;
uses not_empty, not_full, clock_state;
code
   if buffer_state = full then not_full.wait end if;

   (* puts the command in the buffer if and only if it is correct according to
      the clock state, see Figure 9.1 *)
   if (clock_state = running) = (command = 'S') then
   (* puts the command *)
      buffer: = command;
      buffer_state: = full; not_empty.send;
   end if;
end deposit;

procedure remove(result command: char);
uses var clock_state, buffer_state;
uses buffer, not_empty, not_full;
code
   case clock_state

   of stopped:
      if buffer_state = empty then not_empty.wait end if;
      command: = buffer;
      if command = 'R' then clock_state: = running end if;

   of running: (* if the buffer is empty it still contains 'R')
      command: = buffer;
      if command = 'S' then clock_state: = stopped end if;

   end case;
      buffer_state: = empty; not_full.send;
end remove;
```

```
code (* initialization *)
    clock_state: = stopped;
    state_buffer: = empty;
end clock_command;
```

- -

```
monitor chrono_command; (* manages a buffer between processes read
                                    and chronometer *)
defines deposit, remove;

  const
    sec5 = 250; (* 1 unit = 20 ms *)

  var
    chrono_state: (initial_stopped, final_stopped, running);

    buffer: char; (* for a command *)
    buffer_state: (empty, full);

  signal
    not_empty, not_full;

procedure deposit (command: char);
uses var buffer, buffer_state;
uses chrono_state, not_empty, not_full;
code
    if buffer_state = full then not_full.wait end if;

    (* puts the command in the buffer if it is correct according to the
       chronometer state, see Figure 9.1 *)
    if (chrono_state = running) # (command = 'C') then
        buffer: = command;
        buffer_state: = full; not_empty.send;
    end if;
end deposit;

procedure remove (result command: char);
uses var buffer, buffer_state, chrono_state;
uses not_empty, not_full;
    var b: boolean; (* for wait with delay *)
```

177

```
code
  case chrono_state

  of initial_stopped:
    if buffer_state = empty then not_empty.wait end if;
    (* removes the command, which must be 'C' *)
      command: = buffer;
    chrono_state: = running;
    buffer_state: = empty; not_full.send;

  of running: (* if the buffer is empty supply the fictious command 'C' *)
    if buffer_state = empty then command: = 'C'
      else command: = buffer end if;
    if command = 'F' then chrono_state: = final_stopped end if;
    buffer_state: = empty; not_full.send;

  of final_stopped:
    if buffer_state = empty then (* wait for at most 5 seconds *)
      not_empty.wait(delay == sec5, timeout =:b)
    end if;
    (* fictious command 'R' returned in every case, without emptying the
      buffer, see Figure 9.12 *)
    command: = 'R'; chrono_state: = initial_stopped;

  end case;
  end remove;

code (* initialization *)
  chrono_state: = initial_stopped;
  buffer_state: = empty
end chrono_command;
```

- -

```
process read; (* uses the monitor keyboard to read a command, puts this
                  either in the monitor clock_command or in the monitor
                  chrono_command *)
uses keyboard, clock_command, chrono_command;
  var ch: char;
code
```

```
loop
    keyboard.read(ch);
    case ch
    of 'S', 'R', 'h', 'm', 's': (* clock command *)
        clock_command.deposit(ch);
    of 'C', 'I', 'F': (* chronometer command *)
        chrono_command.deposit(ch);
    else (* ignore the command *)
    end case;
    end loop;
end read;
```

- -

```
module hmsc_operations; (* sets, updates and measures digital time to 1/
                           100 sec; used by clock and chronometer every
                           time any change is needed *)
defines
    (* types *) t_time, (* procedures *) initialize, initialize_cents,
    advance_hours, advance_min, advance_sec, plus_one_unit, plus_n_sec,
    convert, equal;
    type t_time = record hours: integer;
                         min:   integer;
                         sec:   integer;
                         cent:  integer end record;


    procedure initialize (result t: t_time); (* initializes time *)
    code
        t.hours: = 0; t.min: = 0; t.sec: = 0; t.cent: = 0;
    end initialize;


    procedure initialize_cents (var t: t_time);
    (* initializes cents of sec of time *)
    code
        t.cent: = 0;
    end initialize_cents;


    procedure advance_hours (var t: t_time); (* increments hours mod 24 *)
    code
        t.hours: = (t.hours + 1) rem 24;
    end advance_hours;
```

179

```
procedure advance_min (var t: t_time); (* increments minutes mod 60
                                              without carry-over to the
                                              hours *)
code
   h.min: = (h.min + 1) rem 60;
end advance_min;


procedure advance_sec (var t: t_time); (* increments seconds mod 60
                                              without carry-over to min *)
code
   t.sec: = (t.sec + 1) rem 60;
end advance_sec;


procedure plus_one_sec (var t: t_time); (* adds one second to the time; a
                                              procedure not exported *)
code
   t.sec: = t.sec + 1;
   if t.sec = 60 then (* increment the minutes *)
      t.min: = t.min + 1; t.sec: = 0;
      if t.min = 60 then (* increment the hours mod 24 *)
         t.hour: = (t.hour + 1) rem 24; t.min: = 0; end if;
   end if;
end plus_one_sec;


procedure plus_n_secs (n: integer; var t: t_time); (* adds n seconds *)
uses plus_one_sec; var i: integer;
code
   i: = 1;
   while i ⩽ n do
      plus_one_sec(t::t);
      i: = i + 1
   end while;
end plus_n_secs;


procedure plus_one_unit (var t: t_time; result sec_carry: boolean);
(* adds 1 unit (= 20 ms = 2 cents) to the time; sec_carry is true if the
   incrementation has affected the seconds *)
uses plus_one_sec;
code
   t.cent: = t.cent + 2; sec_carry: = t.cent = 100;
   if sec_carry then (* increment the seconds *)
      plus_one_sec(t::t); t.cent: = 0 end if;
```

180

```
end plus_one_unit;

procedure convert (t:t_time; cents:boolean; result str: t_string_11);
(* converts a time into a string of characters for display; if cents is true
   then hundredth of seconds are shown, if false these are ignored *)
code
   str: = 'HH:MM:SS   ';
   str[1]: = chr(t.hours div 10 + ord('0'));
   str[2]: = chr(t.hours rem 10 + ord('0'));
   str[4]: = chr(t.min   div 10 + ord('0'));
   str[5]: = chr(t.min   rem 10 + ord('0'));
   str[7]: = chr(t.sec   div 10 + ord('0'));
   str[8]: = chr(t.sec   rem 10 + ord('0'));

   if cents then
      str[9]: = '.';
      str[10]: = chr(t.cent div 10 + ord('0'));
      str[11]: = chr(t.cent rem 10 + ord ('0'));
   end if
end convert;

function equal (t1, t2: t_time): boolean; (* tests the equality of two times *)
code
   equal: = (t1.hours = t2.hours) and (t1.min = t2.min) and (t1.sec = t2.sec)
      and (t1.cent = t2.cent)
end equal;

end hmsc_operations;
```

- -

```
monitor timebase;
defines unit_wait;

   signal s; (* a signal cannot be declared in a procedure *)

   procedure unit_wait; (* suspends the calling process for one unit *)
   uses s; var b: boolean;
   code
      s.wait (delay == 1, timeout =:b);
   end unit_wait;
```

end timebase;

- -

monitor display; (* manages a buffer between clock/chronometer (producer processes) and write (consumer); each buffer will hold one message *)
defines deposit_clocktime, deposit_chronotime, remove;

  var
    clocktime: t_string_11; (* buffer between clock and write processes *)
    chronotime: t_string_11; (* buffer between chronometer and write processes *)
    clockbuffer_state, chronobuffer_state: (empty, full);

  signal
    not_empty; (* at least one buffer is not empty *)

  procedure deposit_clocktime (str: t_string 11);
  (* puts the string 'str' in the buffer, whatever the state of this; clocktime not displayed can be ignored *)
  uses var clocktime, clockbuffer_state; **uses** not_empty;
  code
    clocktime: = str;
    clockbuffer_state: = full; not_empty.send;
  end deposit_clocktime;

  procedure deposit_chronotime (str: t_string_11); (* as for clocktime *)
  uses var chronotime, chronobuffer_state; **uses** not_empty;
  code
    chronotime: = str;
    chronobuffer_state: = full; not_empty.send;
  end deposit_chronotime;

  procedure remove (**result** str: t_string_11; **result** destination: t_dest);
  (* takes from the buffer a string corresponding either to the time of day, for the clock, or to a time interval, for the chronometer; the chronometer has priority *)
  uses var clockbuffer_state, chronobuffer_state;
  uses clocktime, chronotime;
  code
    (* waits until at least one buffer is full *)

182

```
    if (clockbuffer_state = empty) and (chronobuffer_state = empty)
      then not_empty.wait end if;
    if chronobuffer_state = full then
      str: = chronotime; chronobuffer_state: = empty;
      destination: = dest_chrono
    else str: = clocktime; clockbuffer_state: = empty; destination: = dest_clock
    end if;
  end remove;


code (* initialization *)
    clockbuffer_state: = empty; chronobuffer_state: = empty;
end display;
```

_ _

```
process clock;
uses clock_command, timebase, hmsc_operations, display;

  var
    clocktime: hmsc_operations.t_time; (* time as measured by the clock *)
    clocktime_string: t_string_11; (* time as a string of characters *)

    displ: boolean; (* is the time to be displayed? *)
    command: char; (* command read *)

code (* initializes the time and displays 00:00:00 *)
  hmsc_operations.initialize (clocktime);
  hmsc_operations.convert(t == clocktime, cents == false, str ==
                          clocktime_string);
  display.deposit_clocktime (clocktime_string);

  loop
    clock_command.remove (command =:command)
    case command

      of 'R': (* R = Restart; clock running *)
        timebase.unit_wait;
        hmsc_operations.plus_one_unit (t :: clocktime, sec_carry =:displ);

      of 'S': (* S = Stop *)
        hmsc_operations.initialize_cents (clocktime);
        displ: = false;
```

```
      of 'h': (* clock stopped *)
         hmsc_operations.advance_hours (clocktime);
         displ: = true;

      of 'm': (* clock stopped *)
         hmsc_operations.advance_min (clocktime);
         displ: = true;

      of 's': (* clock stopped *)
         hmsc_operations.advance_sec (clocktime);
         displ: = true
      end case;
      if displ then
         hmsc_operations.convert (t == clocktime, cents == false, str ==
                                  clocktime_string);
         display.deposit_clocktime (clocktime_string);
      end if;
   end loop
end clock;
```

- -

```
process chronometer;
uses chrono_command, timebase, hmsc_operations, display;

   var
      chronotime: hmsc_operations.t_time; (* time interval measured by the
                                           chronometer *)
      chronotime_string: t_string_11: (* chronotime as string of chars *)

      intertime: boolean; (* true if intermediate time is to be displayed *)
      end_intertime: hmsc_operations.t_time; (* instant corresponding to end
                                              of display of intermediate
                                              time *)

      displ: boolean; (* is the time to be displayed? *)
      cents: boolean; (* are cents to be displayed? *)

      command: char; (* command read *)

   code
      command: = 'R'; (* initializes and displays chronotime below *)
```
184

```
loop
  case command

    of 'R': (* fictious command: reinitialization *)
      hmsc_operations.initialize (chronotime);
      intertime: = false;
      displ: = true; cents: = false;

    of 'C': (* chronometer running *)
      timebase.unit_wait;
      hmsc_operations.plus_one_unit (t :: chronotime, sec_carry =: displ);
      if intertime then (* is display of intermediate time finished? *)
        intertime: = not hmsc_operations.equal (t1 ==chronotime,
                                                 t2 ==end_intertime);
        (* display suppressed during intermediate time; display on
           otherwise *)
          displ: = not intertime;
          cents: = false
      end if;

    of 'I': (* intermediate time; chronometer running *)
      intertime: = true; (* end_intertime: = chronotime + 3 secs *)
      end_intertime: = chronotime;
      hmsc_operations.plus_n_secs (n == 3, t :: end_intertime);
      (* display time to 1/100 sec *)
      displ: = true; cents: = true;

    of 'F': (* display final time to 1/100 sec *)
      displ: = true; cents: = true

  end case;

  if displ then
    hmsc_operations.convert (t ==chronotime, cents ==cents, str ==
                             chronotime_string);
    display.deposit_chronotime (chronotime_string)
  end if;

  chrono_command.remove (command =: command)
end loop;
end chronometer;
```

- -

```
monitor[4] screen; (* manages the screen at the terminal *)
defines write;

type
   bits = (b0, b1, b2, b3, b4, b5, interr, ready, b8, b9, b10, b11, b12, b13, b14,
         b15);
   state = set of bits;

var
   screen_status at 177564B: state;
   screen_data at 177566B: char;

signal
   interrupt [64B];

procedure write (c: char); (* writes character c on the screen *)
uses var screen_status, screen_data; uses interrupt;
code
   if ready not in screen_status then (* wait until the interface is ready *)
      screen_status: = screen_status + state(interr);
      interrupt.wait;
      screen_status: = screen_status – state(interr);
   end if;
   screen_data: = c (* writes character c *)
end write;


end screen;
```

- -

```
process write; (* takes a string of characters from the display buffer and
               writes it on the screen; clocktime is displayed on the first
               line, chronometer time on the second. The display has
               been made simple deliberately, so as to avoid irrelevant
               complications. *)
uses display, screen;

const escape = 33C; line_feed = 12C;

var
   str: t_string_11; (* string taken from the buffer *)
   destination: t_dest; (* destination: clock or chronometer *)
```

186

```
procedure write_string (s: string); (* displays the string *)
uses screen; var i: integer;
code
   i: = 1;
   while i ⩽ length(s) do
      screen.write (s[i]);
      i: = i + 1;
   end while;
end write_string;


code (* for process write *)
   (* clears the screen *)
      screen.write (escape); screen.write('v');
   loop
      display.remove (str =: str, destination =: destination);
      (* puts the cursor on the first line, ready for the clock *)
         screen.write (escape); screen.write ('H');
      if destination = dest_clock then
         (* puts cursor on second line *)
         screen.write (line_feed);
      end if;
      write_string (str);
   end loop;
end write;
```

- -

```
end clock_chronometer;
```

Appendix 3

SOLUTION OF THE CLOCK/ CHRONOMETER PROBLEM IN MODULA-2

The Modula-2 solution consists of 15 modules: seven definition modules, seven corresponding implementation modules and one module that forms the main program; each of these is compiled separately. They are given here in the following order, first all the definitions and then all the implementations:

SignalKernel
Keyboard
ClockCommand
ChronoCommand
HmscOperations
Display
Screen
ClockChronometer (the main program)

Again, input/output is given in terms of the PDP-11.

DEFINITION MODULE SignalKernel;

EXPORT QUALIFIED
    Signal, Wait, Send, WaitDelay, InitSignal, WaitInterrupt,
    CreateProcess, StartSystem;

TYPE Signal;

PROCEDURE Wait (s: Signal);

PROCEDURE Send (s: Signal);

PROCEDURE WaitDelay (s:Signal; delay:CARDINAL);
    (* waits for a signal, for at most the time given by the delay stated; for
       PDP-11, 1 unit of time = 20 msec *)

188

PROCEDURE Delay (delay: CARDINAL);
   (* suspends a process for the delay stated *)

PROCEDURE InitSignal (VAR s: Signal);
   (* initializes a signal *)

PROCEDURE WaitInterrupt (vector: CARDINAL);
   (* suspends the calling process waiting for an interrupt using the vector
    given as parameter *)

PROCEDURE CreateProcess (P:PROC; StackSize: CARDINAL);
   (* creates a process that executes procedure P; the second parameter
    gives the size of the stack needed by this process *)

PROCEDURE StartSystem;
   (* initiates execution of the processes created by CreateProcess *)

END SignalKernel.

DEFINITION MODULE Keyboard;
   (* handles the terminal keyboard *)

EXPORT QUALIFIED Read;

   PROCEDURE Read (VAR c: CHAR);
   (* reads a character from the keyboard *)

END Keyboard.

DEFINITION MODULE ClockCommand;
   (* manages a buffer between processes Read and Clock *)

EXPORT QUALIFIED Deposit, Remove;

   PROCEDURE Deposit (command: CHAR);

   PROCEDURE Remove (VAR comand: CHAR);

```
END ClockCommand.
```

```
DEFINITION MODULE ChronoCommand;
    (* manages a buffer between processes Read and Chronometer *)

EXPORT QUALIFIED Deposit, Remove;

    PROCEDURE Deposit (command: CHAR);

    PROCEDURE Remove (VAR command: CHAR);

END ChronoCommand.
```

```
DEFINITION MODULE HmscOperations;
    (* sets, updates and measures digital time to 1/100 sec; used by Clock
      and Chronometer every time any change is needed *)

EXPORT QUALIFIED
    tTime, tString11, Initialize, InitializeCents, AdvanceHours, AdvanceMin,
    AdvanceSec, PlusOneUnit, PlusNsecs, Convert, Equal;

TYPE tString11 = ARRAY[0 .. 10] OF CHAR;
    (* string of 11 characters for the time in the form HH:MM:SS.CC, where
      CC gives the hundredths of a second *)

    tTime = RECORD
                hours, min, sec, cent: CARDINAL
            END
            (* transparent export, because in Modula-2 opaque export is
              allowed only for pointers *)
```

```
PROCEDURE Initialize (VAR t: tTime);
(* initializes time to zero *)

PROCEDURE InitializeCents (VAR t: tTime);
(* initializes cents to zero *)
```

PROCEDURE AdvanceHours (VAR t: tTime);
(* increments hours mod 24 *)

PROCEDURE AdvanceMin(VAR t: tTime);
(* increments minutes mod 60, without carry-over to hours *)

PROCEDURE AdvanceSec(VAR t: tTime);
(* increments seconds mod 60, without carry-over to minutes *)

PROCEDURE PlusNsecs(n: CARDINAL; VAR t: tTime);
(* adds n seconds to the time *)

PROCEDURE PlusOneUnit(VAR t: tTime; VAR carrySec: BOOLEAN);
(* adds 1 unit (20 ms = 2 cents) to the time; carrySec is true if the
  incrementation has modified the seconds *)

PROCEDURE Convert(t: tTime; cents: BOOLEAN; VAR string: tString11);
(* converts a time to a character string for display; cents are converted if
  cents = true, otherwise are ignored *)

PROCEDURE Equal(t1, t2: tTime): BOOLEAN;
(* tests for equality of times t1, t2 *)

END HmscOperations.

DEFINITION MODULE Display;
(* manages a buffer between Clock/Chronometer (producers) and Write
  (consumer) *)
FROM HmscOperations IMPORT tString11;

EXPORT QUALIFIED tDest, DepositClocktime, DepositChronotime, Remove;

  TYPE tDest = (destClock, destChrono);
  (* transparent export, used by Write to find whether a character string
    corresponds to time of day for the clock or to a measured time interval
    for the chronometer *)

  PROCEDURE DepositClocktime (string: tString11);
  (* called by Clock *)

```
      PROCEDURE DepositChronotime (string: tString11);
      (* called by Chronometer *)
      PROCEDURE Remove (VAR string: tString; VAR destination: tDest);
      (* called by Write *)
END Display.
```

```
DEFINITION MODULE Screen;
(* handles the terminal screen *)
EXPORT QUALIFIED Write;

      PROCEDURE Write(c: CHAR);
      (* writes the character c on the screen *)

END Screen.
```

```
MODULE ClockChronometer;
(* the main program *)
FROM SignalKernel IMPORT Delay, CreateProcess, StartSystem;
IMPORT Keyboard, ClockCommand, ChronoCommand, HmscOperations,
          Display, Screen;
```

- -

```
PROCEDURE Read;
(* code for process Read; uses Keyboard to read in a command, puts this
      command in one or other of the modules ClockCommand,
      ChronoCommand *)

VAR ch: CHAR; (* the command read *)
BEGIN
   LOOP
      Keyboard.Read(ch);
      CASE ch OF

      'S', 'R', 'h', 'm', 's': (* clock command *)
         ClockCommand.Deposit(ch) |

      'C', 'I', 'F': (* chronometer command *)
         ChronoCommand.Deposit(ch)
```

```
      ELSE (* ignore the command *)

      END (* CASE *)
   END (* LOOP *)
END Read;
```

- -

```
PROCEDURE Clock; (* code for process Clock *)

   CONST
      cents = FALSE; (* no cents in the clock time *)

   VAR
      clocktime: HmscOperations.tTime; (* time as measured by the clock *)
      clocktimeString: HmscOperations.tString11; (* time as a string of
                                                     characters *)
      command: CHAR; (* command read in *)
      displ: BOOLEAN; (* is the time to be displayed on the screen? *)

BEGIN (* initializes time and displays 00:00:00 *)
   HmscOperations.Initialize(clocktime);
   HmscOperations.Convert (clocktime, cents, clocktimeString);
   Display.DepositClocktime (clocktimeString);

   LOOP
      ClockCommand.Remove(command);

      CASE command OF

      'R': (* clock running *)
         Delay(1); (* wait one unit of time *)
         HmscOperations.PlusOneUnit (clocktime, displ) |

      'S': (* stop *)
         HmscOperations.InitializeCents (clocktime);
         displ: = FALSE |

      'h': (* clock stopped *)
         HmscOperations.AdvanceHours (clocktime);
         displ: = TRUE |
```

```
        'm': (* clock stopped *)
        HmscOperations.AdvanceMin (clocktime);
        displ: = TRUE |

        's': (* clock stopped *)
          HmscOperations.AdvanceSec (clocktime);
          displ: = TRUE

        END (* CASE *);
        IF displ THEN
          HmscOperations.Convert (clocktime, cents, clocktimeString);
          Display.DepositClocktime (clocktimeString);
        END (* IF *)
      END (* LOOP *)
  END Clock;
```

- -

```
PROCEDURE Chronometer; (* code for process Chronometer *)

  VAR
      chronotime: HmscOperations.tTime; (* time interval measured by the
                                          chronometer *)
      chronotimeString: HmscOperations.tString; (* chronotime as character
                                                   string *)

      intertime: BOOLEAN; (* is intermediate time to be displayed? *)
      endIntertime: HmscOperations.tTime; (* instant corresponding to end of
                                            display of intermediate time *)

      displ: BOOLEAN; (* is the time to be displayed on the screen? *)
      cents: BOOLEAN; (* are cents to be displayed? *)

      command: CHAR; (* command read in *)

BEGIN (* Chronometer *)
  command: = 'R'; (* causes initialization and display of chronotime *)

  LOOP
    CASE command OF
```

```
'R' (* fictious reinitialization command *)
   HmscOperations.Initialize (chronotime);
   displ: = TRUE; cents: = FALSE; intertime: = FALSE |


'C': (* chronometer running *)
   (* wait one unit of time *)
      Delay(1);
      HmscOperations.PlusOneUnit(chronotime, displ);
   (* handling of possible intermediate time *)
      IF intertime THEN
         (* has the end of the display been reached? *)
            intertime: = NOT HmscOperations.Equal (chronotime,
                                                   endIntertime);
         (* display suppressed during intermediate time; display on
            otherwise *)
            displ: = NOT intertime;
            cents: = FALSE
      END |


'I': (* intermediate time *)
   intertime: = TRUE;
   (* endIntertime: = chronotime + 3 seconds *)
      endIntertime: = chronotime;
      HmscOperations.PlusNsecs (3, endIntertime);
   (* inter. time displayed to 1/100 sec. *)
      displ: = TRUE; cents: = TRUE |


'F': (* final time to be displayed, to 1/100 secs. *)
   displ: = TRUE; cents: = TRUE


END (* CASE *);


IF displ THEN
   HmscOperations.Convert (chronotime, cents, chronotimeString);
   Display.DepositChronotime (chronotimeString);
END;


ChronoCommand.Remove (command);


   END (* LOOP *)
END Chronometer;
```

195

```
PROCEDURE Write;
(* code for process Write: takes a character string from the Display buffer
    and writes it on the screen; the clock is displayed on the first line, the
    chronometer on the second *)
    CONST
        escape = 33C; lineFeed = 12C;
    VAR
        string: HmscOperations.tString11; (* string taken from the Display
                                                        buffer *)
        destination: Display.tDest; (* for the clock or the chronometer *)

    PROCEDURE WriteString (string: ARRAY OF CHAR);
    (* writes the string on the screen *)
        VAR i: CARDINAL;
    BEGIN
        FOR i: = 0 to HIGH (string) DO
            Screen.Write (string[i])
        END
    END WriteString;

BEGIN (* Write *)
    (* clear the screen *)
    Screen.Write (escape); Screen.Write('v');
    LOOP
        Display.Remove (string, destination);
        (* puts the cursor on the first line, ready for the clock *)
            Screen.Write (escape); Screen.Write ('H');
        IF destination = Display.destChrono THEN
            Screen.Write (lineFeed) (* cursor on second line *)
        END;
        WriteString (string)
    END (* LOOP *)
END Write;
```

```
BEGIN (* start of program *)
    CreateProcess (Read          ,2000);
    CreateProcess (Clock         ,2000);
    CreateProcess (Chronometer ,2000);
```

```
CreateProcess (Write        ,2000);
StartSystem
END ClockChronometer.
```

```
IMPLEMENTATION MODULE SignalKernel [7];
  (* priority 7 ensures mutual exclusion *)
FROM SYSTEM IMPORT
  ADDRESS, PROCESS, NEWPROCESS, TRANSFER, IOTRANSFER, LISTEN;
FROM Storage IMPORT ALLOCATE;


TYPE
  PtPrssDesc   = POINTER TO ProcessDesc;
  Signal       = PtPrssDesc;
  ProcessDesc = RECORD
                 next: PtPrssDesc; (* next in circular list of processes *)
                 succ, pred: PtPrssDesc; (* successor/predecessor in list
                                            of processes waiting for a
                                            signal *)
                 ready: BOOLEAN; (* process state *)
                 delay: CARDINAL; (* waiting time, used by Delay *)
                 prss: PROCESS (* to designate the process *)
               END;
VAR
  CurrentProcess :PtPrssDesc;
  Idle           :PtPrssDesc;
  IdleCreation   :BOOLEAN; (* TRUE during creation of process Idle,
                              otherwise FALSE *)


PROCEDURE Empty (s: Signal): BOOLEAN; (* indicates whether signal's
                                         list is empty *)
BEGIN
  RETURN s = s↑.succ; (* cf Figure 9.17 *)
END Empty;


PROCEDURE RemoveHead (header: Signal; VAR removed: PtPrssDesc);
(* removes the process at the head of the (non-empty) list of the signal *)
VAR
  first: PtPrssDesc;
    (* the process at the head of the list after the removal *)
BEGIN
  removed: = header↑.succ; first: = removed↑.succ;
```

```
        (* take the process from the list *)
            header↑.succ: = first; first↑.pred: = header;
        (* state that it is not in a list *)
            removed↑.succ: = removed; removed↑.pred: = removed;
    END RemoveHead;


    PROCEDURE InsertTail (header: Signal; toBeInserted: PtPrssDesc);
    (* puts a process at the tail of the signal's list *)
    VAR
        last: PtPrssDesc;
            (* the process at the tail of the list before the insertion *)
    BEGIN
        last: = header↑.pred;
        (* adds the process to the list *)
            last↑.succ: = toBeInserted; toBeInserted↑.pred: = last;
            toBeInserted↑.succ: = header; header↑.pred: = toBeInserted;
    END InsertTail;


    PROCEDURE Remove (toBeRemoved: PtPrssDesc);
    (* removes a process from the signal's list in which it is residing *)
    VAR
        successor, predecessor: PtPrssDesc; (* of the process to be removed *)
    BEGIN
        successor: = toBeRemoved↑.succ; predecessor: = toBeRemoved↑.pred;
        (* removes the process from the list *)
            predecessor↑.succ: = successor; successor↑.pred: = predecessor;
        (* states that the process is not in any list *)
            toBeRemoved↑.succ: = toBeRemoved;
            toBeRemoved↑.pred: = toBeRemoved;
    END Remove;


    PROCEDURE NextProcess (VAR CurrentProcess: PtPrssDesc);
    (* selects a process for execution *)
    VAR
        p: PtPrssDesc;
    BEGIN
        p: = CurrentProcess;
        REPEAT p: = p↑.next UNTIL p↑.ready OR (p = CurrentProcess);
        IF NOT p↑.ready THEN
            (* no process has been found that is ready, so Idle is chosen *)
            p: = Idle;
```

198

```
    END;
    CurrentProcess: = p (* process selected *)
END NextProcess;

PROCEDURE Wait (s: Signal);
VAR blocked: PtPrssDesc;
BEGIN
    (* process executing Wait is blocked *)
        blocked: = CurrentProcess; blocked↑.ready: = FALSE;
    IF s = NIL THEN
        (* pseudo-signal used by procedure Delay *)
    ELSE (* put the process at the end of the signal' list *)
        InsertTail (s, blocked);
    END;
    (* activate a new process *)
        NextProcess (CurrentProcess);
        TRANSFER (blocked↑.prss, CurrentProcess↑.prss);
END Wait;

PROCEDURE Delay (delay: CARDINAL);
(* suspends a process for the time stated; 1 unit = 20 msec on PDP 11 *)
BEGIN
    CurrentProcess↑.delay: = delay; Wait(NIL);
END Delay;

PROCEDURE WaitDelay (s: Signal; delay: CARDINAL);
(* waits for a signal, for the stated delay time at most *)
BEGIN
    CurrentProcess↑.delay: = delay; Wait(s);
END WaitDelay;

PROCEDURE Send (s: Signal);
VAR
    awakened: PtPrssDesc;
    sender: PtPrssDesc; (* the process that sends the signal *)
BEGIN
    IF NOT Empty(s) THEN (* the signal is expected *)
        sender: = CurrentProcess;
        (* remove the process from the head of the list *)
            RemoveHead (s, awakened);
        (* cancel any possible delay *)
```

```
            awakened↑.delay: = 0;
        (* execute the awakened process *)
            awakened↑.ready: = TRUE; CurrentProcess: = awakened;
            TRANSFER (sender↑.prss, awakened↑.prss);
    END;
END Send;


PROCEDURE InitSignal (VAR s: Signal);
(initializes a signal *)
BEGIN
    NEW(s); (* allocates the list header *)
    (* initialize an empty circular list *)
        s↑.succ: = s; s↑.pred: = s;
END InitSignal;


PROCEDURE WaitInterrupt (vector: CARDINAL);
(* suspends the calling process, waiting for an interrupt using the vector
    given as parameter *)
VAR
    p: PROCESS:
    WaitingInterrupt: PtPrssDesc; (* process waiting for the interrupt *)
BEGIN
    (* block the calling process *)
        WaitingInterrupt: = CurrentProcess;
        WaitingInterrupt↑.ready: = FALSE;
    (* select the next process to execute *)
        NextProcess (currentProcess);

    (* activate the current process; at the instant of the interrupt p will
        designate the interrupted process *)
        p: = CurrentProcess↑.prss;
        IOTRANSFER (WaitingInterrupt↑.prss, p, vector);
        CurrentProcess↑.prss: = p;

    (* the process awakened by the interrupt becomes the current process *)
        WaitingInterrupt↑.ready: = TRUE;
        CurrentProcess: = WaitingInterrupt;
END WaitInterrupt;


PROCEDURE CreateProcess (P: PROC; StackSize: CARDINAL);
(* creates a process that executes procedure P; StackSize gives the size of
    the stack needed by the process *)
```

```
VAR
  a: ADDRESS;
  created: PtPrssDesc; (* the new process *)
BEGIN
  (* allocate storage for the stack *)
    ALLOCATE (a, StackSize)
  (* allocate storage for the descriptor *)
    NEW(created);
  NEWPROCESS (P, a, StackSize, created↑.prss);

  (* initialize the process descriptor *)
    created↑.delay: = 0;
    created↑.ready: = NOT IdleCreation; (* ready = FALSE only for Idle *)
    (* process not in any list *)
      created↑.succ: = created; created↑.pred: = created;

  (* put the new process in the process list *)
    IF IdleCreation THEN
    (* Idle is the first process created *)
      Idle: = created; CurrentProcess: = Idle;
    ELSE
    (* new process is put at the head of the list *)
      created↑.next: = CurrentProcess; CurrentProcess: = created;
    END;
  (* maintain the circularity of the list; Idle is always at the tail *)
    Idle↑.next: = CurrentProcess;
END CreateProcess;


PROCEDURE Idle;
(* code for Idle process *)
BEGIN
  LOOP
    LISTEN (* lowers priority, so that all interrupts are allowed *)
  END
END Idle;


PROCEDURE DecrementDelay (VAR awakened: PtPrssDesc);
(* scans the process list, reduces all delays by one unit and awakens a
    process whose delay has become 0; if no process is awakened the
    parameter takes the value NIL, otherwise it gives the last process
    awakened *)
```

```
    VAR p: PtPrssDesc;
    BEGIN
      awakened: = NIL;
      p: = CurrentProcess; (* which is active, so delay = 0 *)
      REPEAT
        p: = p↑.next;
        IF p↑.delay # 0 THEN
          p↑.delay: = p↑.delay – 1;
          IF p↑.delay = 0 THEN
            (* remove the process from the list of the signal in which it may be
               residing *)
            Remove(p);
            awakened: = p; awakened↑.ready: = TRUE;
          END;
        END;
      UNTIL p = CurrentProcess;
    END DecrementDelay;


    PROCEDURE StartSystem;
    (* engages the clock and initiates execution of CurrentProcess; the
       procedure DecrementDelay is called at each clock interrupt *)
    CONST
      clockVector = 100B; (* system clock vector *)
      interr = 6; (* interrupt bit in clock status register *)
    VAR
      awakened: PtPrssDesc;
      clock, p: PROCESS;
      clockReg[177546B]: BITSET; (* clock status register *)
    BEGIN
      (* enables clock interrupts *)
        INCL(clockReg, interr);
      LOOP (* activates CurrentProcess; at the moment of the interrupt,
        p will designate the interrupted process *)
          p: = CurrentProcess↑.prss;
          IOTRANSFER (clock, p, clockVector);
          CurrentProcess↑.prss: = p;

        (* activates the process whose delay becomes 0 *)
          DecrementDelay (awakened);
          IF awakened # NIL THEN CurrentProcess: = awakened END;
      END (* LOOP *)
    END StartSystem;
```

```
BEGIN (* initialization *)
  IdleCreation: = TRUE;
  CreateProcess (Idle, 128);
  IdleCreation: = FALSE;
END SignalKernel.
```

```
IMPLEMENTATION MODULE Keyboard [4]; (* keyboard interrupt has priority
                                            4 *)
FROM SignalKernel IMPORT WaitInterrupt;

  CONST
    ready = 7; (* 'ready' bit of keyboard status register *)
    interr = 6; (* 'interrupt' bit *)
    interVector = 60B;

  VAR
    keyboardStatus [177560B]: BITSET;
    keyboardData [177562B]: CHAR;

  PROCEDURE Read(VAR c: CHAR); (* reads a character from the
                                        keyboard *)
  BEGIN
    IF NOT (ready IN keyboardStatus) THEN
    (* wait for a character *)
      INCL (keyboardStatus, interr);
      WaitInterrupt (interVector);
      EXCL (keyboardStatus, interr);
    END;
    (* read a character *)
      c: = keyboardData;
    (* suppress parity bit *)
      IF ORD(c) >= 200B THEN c: = CHR(ORD(c) - 200B) END;
  END Read;

END Keyboard.
```

```
IMPLEMENTATION MODULE ClockCommand [7]; (* priority 7 ensures
                                        mutual exclusion *)
FROM SignalKernel IMPORT Signal, InitSignal, Wait, Send;
  VAR
    clockState: (stopped, running);

    buffer: CHAR; (* for a command *)
    bufferState: (empty, full);

    notEmpty, notFull: Signal;

  PROCEDURE Deposit (command: CHAR);
  BEGIN
    IF bufferState = full THEN Wait (notFull) END;
    (* put a command in the buffer only if legal: see Figure 9.1 *)
      IF (clockState = running) = (command = 'S') THEN
        buffer: = command;
        bufferState: = full; Send (notEmpty)
      END;
  END Deposit;

  PROCEDURE Remove (VAR command: CHAR);
  BEGIN
    CASE clockState OF
    stopped:
      IF bufferState = empty THEN Wait (notEmpty) END;
      command: = buffer;
      IF command = 'R' THEN clockState: = running END;
      bufferState: = empty; Send (notFull) |

    running:
      (* if bufferState = empty then buffer still contains 'R' *)
      command: = buffer;
      IF command = 'S' THEN clockState: = stopped END;
      bufferState: = empty; Send (notFull);
    END;
  END Remove;

BEGIN (* initialization *)
  InitSignal (notEmpty); InitSignal (notFull);
  clockState: = stopped; bufferState: = empty;
END ClockCommand.
```

IMPLEMENTATION MODULE ChronoCommand [7]; (* priority 7 for mutual exclusion *)
FROM SignalKernel IMPORT Signal, InitSignal, Wait, WaitDelay, Send;

CONST fiveSecs = 250; (* 1 unit of time = 20 msec *)

VAR
  chronoState: (initialStopped, running, finalStopped);

  buffer: CHAR;
  bufferState: (empty, full); (* buffer can contain at most one command *)
  notEmpty, notFull: Signal;

PROCEDURE Deposit (command: CHAR);
BEGIN
  IF bufferState = full THEN Wait(notFull) END;
  (* put a command in the buffer only if it is legal; see Figure 9.1 *)
    IF (chronoState = running) # (command = 'C') THEN
      buffer: = command;
      bufferState: = full; Send(notEmpty)
    END;
END Deposit;

PROCEDURE Remove (VAR command: CHAR);
BEGIN
    CASE chronoState OF

    initialStopped:
      (* wait for a command, which must be 'C' *)
        IF bufferState = empty THEN Wait (notEmpty) END;
        command: = buffer;
      chronoState: = running;
      bufferState: = empty; Send (notFull) |

  running:
    (* if buffer is empty a fictitious 'C' is given *)
      IF bufferState = empty THEN command: = 'C'
      ELSE command: = buffer END;
    IF command = 'F' THEN chronoState: = finalStopped END;
    bufferState: = empty; Send (notFull) |

205

```
        finalStopped:
            IF bufferState = empty THEN
            (* wait for at most 5 seconds *)
                WaitDelay (notEmpty, fiveSecs) END;
            (* returns fictitious 'R' without emptying the buffer, see Figure 9.12 *)
                command: = 'R';
            (* reinitializes chrono state *)
                chronoState: = initialStopped;


        END (* CASE *)
    END Remove;


    BEGIN (* initialization *)
        InitSignal (notEmpty); InitSignal (notFull);
        bufferState: = empty; chronoState: = initialStopped;
    END ChronoCommand.
```

```
IMPLEMENTATION MODULE HmscOperations;
(* sets, updates and measures digital time, expressed as hours, minutes,
    seconds and cents (hundredths of a second)

TYPE
    tTime = RECORD  hours, min, sec, cent: CARDINAL
            END;
    tString11 = ARRAY [0 .. 10] OF CHAR; *)

PROCEDURE initialize(VAR t: tTime); (* initializes time *)
BEGIN
    t.hours: = 0; t.min: = 0; t.sec: = 0; t.cent: = 0;
END initialize;

PROCEDURE initializeCents (VAR t: tTime);
    t.cent: = 0
END initializeCents;

PROCEDURE Equal (t1, t2: tTime): BOOLEAN; (* tests equality of two lines *)
BEGIN
    RETURN (t1.hours = t2.hours) AND (t1.min = t2.min) AND
            (t1.sec = t2.sec) AND (t1.cent = t2.cent)
END Equal;
```

206

```
PROCEDURE AdvanceHours (VAR t: tTime); (* increments hours mod 24 *)
BEGIN
   t.hours: = (t.hours + 1) MOD 24;
END AdvanceHours;


PROCEDURE AdvanceMin (VAR t: tTime); (* advances minutes mod 60
                                      without carry to hours *)
BEGIN
   t.mins: = (t.mins + 1) MOD 60;
END AdvanceMin;


PROCEDURE AdvanceSec (VAR t: tTime); (* advances seconds mod 60
                                      without carry to minutes *)
BEGIN
   t.sec: = (t.sec + 1) MOD 60;
END AdvanceSec;


PROCEDURE PlusOneSecond (VAR t: tTime) (* adds one second to the time,
                          with carry to minutes and hours if necessary *)
BEGIN
   AdvanceSec(t);
   IF t.sec = 0 THEN AdvanceMin(t);
      IF t.min = 0 THEN AdvanceHours(t) END;
   END;
END PlusOneSecond;


PROCEDURE PlusNsecs (n: CARDINAL; VAR t: tTime); (* adds n seconds to
                                                  time *)
VAR i: CARDINAL;
BEGIN
   FOR i: = 1 TO n DO PlusOneSecond(t) END;
END PlusNsecs;


PROCEDURE PlusOneUnit (VAR t: tTime; VAR carrySec: BOOLEAN);
(* adds one unit (2 cents) to time; carrySec = TRUE if this affects secs *)
BEGIN
   t.cent: = (t.cent + 2) MOD 100;
   carrySec: = (t.cent = 0);
   IF carrySec THEN PlusOneSecond (t) END;
END PlusOneUnit;
```

```
    PROCEDURE Convert (t: tTime; cents: BOOLEAN; VAR string: tString11);
    (* converts time to a character string for display; if cents = TRUE, cents are
        displayed, otherwise are ignored *)
    VAR figure: ARRAY [0 .. 9] OF CHAR;
    BEGIN
        string: = 'HH:MM:SS   '; figure: = '0123456789';
        (* convert hours *)
            string [0]: = figure [t.hours DIV 10];
            string [1]: = figure [t.hours MOD 10];
        (* convert minutes *)
            string [3]: = figure [t.min DIV 10];
            string [4]: = figure [t.min MOD 10];
        (* convert seconds *)
            string [6]: = figure [t.sec DIV 10];
            string [7]: = figure [t.sec MOD 10];
        IF cents THEN
        (* convert cents if required *)
            string [08]: = '.';
            string [09]: = figure [t.cent DIV 10];
            string [10]: = figure [t.cent MOD 10];
        END;
    END Convert;


    END HmscOperations.
```

```
    IMPLEMENTATION MODULE Display [7];
    (* manages a buffer between Clock/Chronometer (producers) and Write
        (consumer); each buffer will hold one message; priority 7 ensures mutual
        exclusion *)
    FROM HmscOperations IMPORT tString11;
    FROM SignalKernel IMPORT Signal, InitSignal, Send, Wait;

    (* TYPE tDest = (destClock, destChrono) *)

    VAR
        clocktime: tString11; (* buffer for clock *)
        chronotime: tString11; (* buffer for chronometer *)
        clockBufferState, chronoBufferState: (empty, full);

        notEmpty: Signal; (* at least one buffer is not empty *)
```

```
PROCEDURE DepositClocktime (string: tString11);
(* puts the clock time in the buffer, even if this is not empty at that instant; a
    previous clocktime, not displayed, is overwritten *)
BEGIN
   clocktime: = string;
   clockBufferState: = full; Send (notEmpty);
END DepositClocktime;


PROCEDURE DepositChronotime (string: tString11);
(* as for DepositClocktime *)
BEGIN
   chronotime: = string;
   chronoBufferState: = full; Send(notEmpty);
END DepositChronotime;


PROCEDURE Remove (VAR string: tString11; VAR destination: tDest);
(* takes a string from the buffer, which corresponds to clocktime if
    destination = destClock, to chronotime if destination = destChrono;
    chronotime has priority *)
BEGIN
   IF (clockBufferState = empty) AND (chronoBufferState = empty) THEN
      Wait (notEmpty)
   END;
   IF chronoBufferState = full THEN destination: = destChrono;
      string: = chronotime; chronoBufferState: = empty;
   ELSE destination: = destClock;
         string: = clocktime; clockBufferState: = empty
   END;
END Remove;


BEGIN (* initialization *)
   InitSignal(notEmpty);
   chronoBufferState: = empty; clockBufferState: = empty;
END Display.
```

```
IMPLEMENTATION MODULE Screen [4];
(* screen interrupt is at priority 4 *)
FROM SignalKernel IMPORT WaitInterrupt;
```

```
CONST
  ready = 7; interr = 6; (* ready/interrupt bits in screen status register *)
  intervector = 64B; (* address of screen interrupt vector *)

VAR screenStatus [177564B]: BITSET;
    screenData[177566B]: CHAR;

PROCEDURE Write (c: CHAR);
(* writes character c on the screen *)
BEGIN
  IF NOT (ready IN screenStatus) THEN (* wait for the interface to become
                                                         ready *)
    INCL (screenStatus, interr);
    WaitInterrupt (intervector);
    EXCL (screenStatus, interr)
  END;
  screenData: = c; (* writes the character c *)
END Write;

END Screen.
```

Appendix 4

SOLUTION OF THE CLOCK/ CHRONOMETER PROBLEM IN ADA

The Ada program consists of ten units, given here in this order:

- specification of the package hmsc_operations (a package is the Ada equivalent of a module)
- procedure clock_chronometer: this forms the main program, and contains the specifications of all the tasks
- package body hmsc_operations
- task body read
- task body clock_command
- task body chrono_command
- task body clock
- task body chronometer
- task body display
- task body write.

Each unit is compiled separately. As before, input/output is in terms relevant to the PDP-11; and the assumption is made that the instruction **delay** system.tick suspends a task until the next interrupt from the system clock arrives, which for this machine is every 20 ms.

Because it uses some low-level concepts, and because an adequate compiler was not available, it has not been possible to test this program.

package hmsc_operations **is**
−− sets, updates and measures digital time (hours, minutes, seconds, cents).
−− used by clock, chronometer each time any change is needed

    type t_time **is private**; −− opaque export

    subtype t_string **is** string(1 .. 11);
    −− string of 11 characters, giving clocktime as HH:MM:SS.CC, where CC
    −− gives the 1/100 secs (cents)

    procedure initialize (t: **out** t_time);
    −− initializes clocktime to 0 hours, 0 min, 0 sec, 0 cents

procedure initialize_cents (t: **in out** t_time);
-- initializes cents to 0

procedure advance_hours (t: **in out** t_time);
-- increments hours mod 24

procedure advance_min (t: **in out** t_time);
-- increments minutes mod 60, without carry to hours

procedure advance_sec (t: **in out** t_time);
-- increments seconds mod 60, without carry to minutes

procedure plus_n_secs (n: natural; t: **in out** t_time);
-- adds n seconds to t

procedure plus_one_unit (t: **in out** t_time; carry_sec: **out** boolean);
-- adds one unit of time (20 ms = 2 cents) to the time; carry_sec is true
-- if the incrementation has affected the seconds

procedure convert (t: **in out** t_time; cents: boolean; str: **out** t_string_11);
-- converts measured time to a character string for display; cents
-- states whether cents are to be converted or ignored

private -- not visible outside the package

   type t_time **is record**
           hours: natural;
           min: natural;
           sec: natural;
           cent: natural;
      end record;
end hmsc_operations;

---

with hmsc_operations; -- package import
use hmsc_operations; -- makes the entities exported by the package directly
                      -- visible

procedure clock_chronometer **is** -- the main program

```
type t_dest is (dest_clock, dest_chrono);
  -- used by task write to decide whether a character string is clocktime
  -- or chronotime

task read is
  entry keyboard_interr;
  for keyboard_interr use at 8#60#;
end read;

task clock_command is -- manages a buffer between read and clock
  entry deposit (command: character);
  entry remove (command: out character);
end clock_command;

task chrono_command is -- manages a buffer between read and
                                chronometer
  entry deposit (command: character);
  entry remove (command: out character);
end chrono_command;

task clock;

task chronometer;

task display is
-- manages a buffer between clock, chronometer
-- (producers) and write (consumer)
  entry deposit_clocktime (str: t_string_11);
  entry deposit_chronotime (str: t_string_11);
  entry remove (str: out t_string_11; destination: out t_dest);
end display;

task write is
  entry screen_interr;
  for screen_interr use at 8#64#;
end write;

-- the bodies of the following tasks are compiled separately:
task body read is separate;
task body clock_command is separate;
task body chrono_command is separate;
```

213

```
task body clock is separate;
task body chronometer is separate;
task body display is separate;
task body write is separate;

begin -- clock_chronometer
    -- start of execution of above tasks
    null; -- the main program terminates only when all the tasks
        -- have terminated: so this program never terminates
end clock_chronometer;
```

```
package body hmsc_operations is -- manages digital time (hours, mins,
                                            secs, cents)

    -- type t_time is record
    --                    hours: natural; min: natural; sec: natural; cent: natural;
    --                    end record;
    --        t_string_11 is string(1 .. 11);

procedure initialize (t: out t_time) is -- initializes time
begin
    t: = (0, 0, 0, 0);
end initialize;

procedure initialize_cents (t: in out t_time) is
begin
    t.cent: = 0;
end initialize_cents;

procedure advance_hours (t: in out t_time) is
begin
    t.hours: = (t.hours + 1) mod 24;
end advance_hours;

procedure advance_min (t: in out t_time) is -- no carry to hours
begin
    t.min: = (t.min + 1) mod 60;
end advance_min;
```

```
procedure advance_sec (t: in out t_time) is -- no carry to minutes
begin
   t.sec: = (t.sec + 1) mod 60;
end advance_sec;


procedure plus_one_second (t: in out t_time) is -- with possible carry
begin
   advance_sec(t);
   if t.sec = 0 then advance_min(t);
      if t.min = 0 then advance_hours(t); end if;
   end if;
end plus_one_second;


procedure plus_n_secs (n: natural; t: in out t_time) is
begin
   for i in 1 .. n loop
      plus_one_second (t);
   end loop;
end plus_n_secs;


procedure plus_one_unit (t: in out t_time; carry_sec: out boolean) is
begin
   t.cent: = (t.cent + 2) mod 100;
   carry_sec: = t.cent = 0;
   if t.cent = 0 then plus_one_sec(t); end if;
end plus_one_unit;


procedure convert (t: in out t_time; cents: boolean; str: out t_string_11) is
   figure: constant string: = '0123456789';
begin
      str: = "00:00:00   ";
      str(1): = figure (t.hours/10);
      str(2): = figure (t.hours mod 10);
      str(4): = figure (t.min/10);
      str(5): = figure (t.min mod 10);
      str(7): = figure (t.sec/10);
      str(8): = figure (t.sec mod 10);
      if cents then str(9): = '.';
                    str(10): = figure (t.cent/10);
                    str(11): = figure (t.cent mod 10);
      end if;
```

```
    end convert;
end hmsc_operations;
```

```
separate (clock_chronometer)
-- unit containing the specification of the task


task body read is -- reads commands from the keyboard

-- const
    ready: constant: = 7; -- 'ready' bit in keyboard status register
    interrupt: constant: = 6; -- 'interrupt' bit

-- type
    type state is array (0 .. 15) of boolean;
    for state'size use 16; -- type state represented by 16 bits (1 word)

-- var
    keyboard_status: state; -- keyboard status register
    for keyboard_status use at #8#177560#;

    keyboard_data: character; -- keyboard data register
    for keyboard_data use at #8#177562#;

    c: character; -- character read from the keyboard

begin
  loop
    if not keyboard_status (ready) then -- wait for a character to be typed
      keyboard_status (interrupt): = true;
      accept keyboard_interr;
      keyboard_status (interrupt): = false;
    end if;

    -- read a character typed on the keyboard, suppress the parity bit
      c: = keyboard_data;
      if character'pos(c) ≥ 8#200# then
        c: = character'val (character'pos(c) - 8#200#);
      end if;
    -- put the command in either the clock or the chronometer buffer, as
      required
      case c is
```

```
      when 'S' | 'R' | 'h' | 'm' | 's' =>
      -- clock command
          clock_command.deposit(c);

      when 'C' | 'I' | 'F' =>
      -- chronometer command
          chrono_command.deposit(c);

      when others => null;
      -- ignore all other characters

      end case;

    end loop;
end read;
```

```
separate (clock_chronometer)
-- unit containing the specification of the task

task body clock_command is
-- manages clock buffer

    type t_clock_state is (stopped, running);
    type t_buffer_state is (empty, full);

    clock_state: t_clock_state;

    buffer: character; -- buffer holds one command
    buffer_state: t_buffer_state;

begin
    clock_state: = stopped; buffer_state: = empty;
    loop
      select
        when buffer_state = empty =>
          accept deposit (command: character) do
            -- put a command in the buffer only if it is correct according to
               the clock state
            if (clock_state = running) = (command = 'S') then
              buffer: = command; buffer_state: = full;
```

```
            end if;
          end deposit;
      or
        when (clock_state = stopped) and (buffer_state = empty) =>
          accept remove (command: out character) do
            command: = buffer; -- takes a command from the buffer
          end remove;
          if buffer = 'R' then clock_state: = running; end if;
          buffer_state: = empty;
      or
        when (clock_state = running) =>
          accept remove (command: out character) do
            -- if buffer_state = empty then buffer contains 'R'
            command: = buffer;
          end remove;
          if buffer = 'S' then clock_state: = stopped; end if;
          buffer_state: = empty;

      end select;
    end loop;
  end clock_command;
```

```
separate (clock_chronometer)
-- unit containing the specification of the task

task body chrono_command is -- manages the chronometer buffer

    type t_chrono_state is (initial_stopped, running, final_stopped);
    type t_buffer_state is (empty, full);

    chrono_state: t_chrono_state;
    buffer: character; -- buffer holds one command
    buffer_state: t_buffer_state;

begin
    chrono_state: = initial_stopped; buffer_state: = empty;
    loop
      select
```

```
    when buffer_state = empty =>
      accept deposit (command: character) do
        -- put a command in the buffer only if it is correct according to
        -- the chronometer state
          if (chrono_state = running) /= (command = 'C') then
            buffer: = command; buffer_state: = full;
          end if;
      end deposit;
  or
    when (chrono_state = initial_stopped) and (buffer_state = full) =>
      accept remove (command: out character) do
        -- command must be 'C'
        command: = buffer;
      end remove;
      -- consequentially restarts chronometer
        chrono_state: = running;
      buffer_state: = empty;
  or
    when (chrono_state = running) =>
      accept remove (command: out character) do
      -- if the buffer is empty a fictitious command 'C' is supplied
        if buffer_state = empty then buffer: = 'C'; end if;
        command: = buffer;
      end remove;
      buffer_state: = empty;
      if buffer = 'F' then chrono_state: = final_stopped; end if;
  or
    when (chrono_state = final_stopped) and (buffer_state = full) =>
      accept remove (command: out character) do
      -- fictitious command 'R', does not empty buffer
        command: = 'R';
      end remove;
      chrono_state: = initial_stopped;
  or
    when (chrono_state = final_stopped) and (buffer_state = empty) =>
      delay 5.0; -- 5 seconds
      accept remove (command: out character) do
        command: = 'R'; -- fictitious 'R'
      end remove;
      chrono_state: = initial_stopped;
```

```
      end select;
    end loop;
  end chrono_command;
```

```
  with hmsc_operations, system; -- packages imported: system is predefined

  use manage_hmsc; -- makes entities exported by the package directly
                   -- visible

  separate (clock_chronometer) -- unit containing task specification

  task body clock is

    clocktime: t_time;
    clocktime_string: t_string_11; -- clocktime as a character string

    displ: boolean; -- whether or not clocktime is to be displayed
    cents: constant boolean: = false; -- cents are never displayed in clocktime

    command: character; -- command read from the keyboard

  begin
    -- initializes clocktime and displays 00:00:00
      initialize (clocktime);
      convert (clocktime, cents, clocktime_string);
      display.deposit_clocktime (clocktime_string);
  loop
      clock_command.remove (command);
      case command is

      when 'R' => -- clock running
        -- waits one unit of time
          delay system.tick;
        plus_one_unit (clocktime, displ);

      when 'S' => -- stop
          initialize_cents (clocktime);
          displ: = false;
```

```
     when 'h' => -- clock stopped
        advance_hours (clocktime);
        displ: = true;

     when 'm' => -- clock stopped
        advance_min (clocktime);
        displ: = true;

     when 's' => -- clock stopped
        advance_sec (clocktime);
        displ: = true;

     when others => null;

     end case;

     if displ then convert (clocktime, cents, clocktime_string);
                  display.deposit_clocktime (clocktime_string);
     end if;

   end loop;
end clock;
```

```
with hmsc_operations, system; -- packages imported, system is predefined
use hmsc_operations; -- makes entities exported by the package directly
                     -- visible

separate (clock_chronometer) -- unit containing task specification

task body chronometer is

   chronotime: t_time;
   chronotime_string: t_string_11;
   intertime: boolean; -- true if intermediate time is to be displayed
   end_intertime: t_time; -- end of display of intermediate time

   displ: boolean; -- true if chronotime is to be displayed
   cents: boolean; -- true if cents are to be displayed

   command: character; -- command read from the keyboard
```

```
 begin
.   command: = 'R'; -- initializes and displays chronotime below

   loop
     case command is

       when 'R' => -- initializes chronotime
         intertime: = false;
         initialize (chronotime);
         displ: = true; cents: = false;

       when 'C' => -- chronometer running
         -- wait one unit of time
           delay system.tick;
         plus_one_unit (chronotime, displ);

         if intertime then -- is display of intermediate time complete?
           intertime: = chronotime ≠ end_intertime;
           -- display inhibited during intermediate time,
           -- resumed at the end of this
             displ: = not intertime;
             cents: = false;
         end if;

       when 'I' => -- intermediate time required
         intertime: = true;
         -- end_intertime: = chronotime + 3 secs
           end_intertime: = chronotime;
           plus_n_secs (3, end_intertime);
         -- display intertime to 1/100 secs
           displ: = true; cents: = true;

       when 'F' => -- displays final time
         displ: = true; cents: = true;

       when others => null;

     end case;
```

```
    if displ then
        convert (chronotime, cents, chronotime_string);
        display.deposit_chronotime (chronotime_string);
    end if;

    chrono_command.remove (command);

  end loop;
end chronometer;
```

```
with hmsc_operations; -- package imported
use hmsc_operations; -- makes entities exported by the package
                     -- directly visible

separate (clock_chronometer)
-- unit containing task specification

task body display is
-- manages a buffer between tasks clock, chronometer (producers) and
-- write (consumer); each buffer will hold one message

  type buffer_state is (empty, full);

  clocktime: t_string_11;
  clocktime_state: buffer_state; -- clock buffer

  chronotime: t_string_11;
  chronotime_state: buffer_state; -- chronometer buffer

begin
  loop
    select

      accept deposit_chronotime (str: t_string_11) do
        -- erases buffer contents: if the time stored has not been displayed
        -- it can be ignored
        chronotime: = str;
      end deposit_chronotime;
      chronotime_state: = full;
```

```
    or
       accept deposit_clocktime (str: t_string_11) do -- same comment
          clocktime: = str;
       end deposit_clocktime;
       clocktime_state: = full;
    or
       when chronotime_state = full =>
          accept remove (str: out t_string_11; destination: out t_dest) do
             str: = chronotime; destination: = dest_chrono;
          end remove;
          chronotime_state: = empty;
    or
       when clocktime_state = full =>
          accept remove (str: out t_string_11; destination: out t_dest) do
             str: = clocktime; destination: = dest_clock;
          end remove;
          clocktime_state: = empty;

    end select;
  end loop;
end display;
```

```
with hmsc_operations;

use hmsc_operations;

separate (clock_chronometer)

task body write is
-- takes a string from the buffer display and writes it on the screen;
-- clocktime is displayed on the first line, chronometer time on the second

   ready: constant: = 7; -- 'ready' bit of screen status register
   interrupt: constant: = 6; -- 'interrupt' bit
   length_11: constant integer: = t_string_11'last; -- length of string

-- type
   type state is array (0 .. 15) of boolean;
   for state'size use 16; -- state represented by 16 bits (1 word)
```

```
-- var
      screen_status: state; -- screen status register
      for screen_status use at 8#177564#;

      screen_data: character; -- screen data register
      for screen_data use at 8#177566#;

      str: t_string_11; -- string taken from the buffer, for display
      destination: t_dest; -- destination of string, clock or chronometer
      to_be_displayed: string (1 .. length_11 + 3); -- string to be displayed
      nb_char: natural; -- number of characters to be displayed

begin
   -- construct the string that will clear the screen
   to_be_displayed(1 .. 2): = ascii.esc & 'v'; -- & means concatenation
   nb_char: = 2;

loop
   -- displays the string to_be_displayed (1 .. nb_char)
      for i in 1 .. nb_char loop -- displays character to_be_dislayed(i)
         if not screen_status (ready) then
            -- wait for screen to become ready
            screen_status (interrupt): = true;
            accept screen_interr;
            screen_status (interrupt): = false;
         end if;
         screen_data: = to_be_displayed(i); -- writes the character
      end loop; -- end of loop on i

   display.remove (str, destination);
   case destination is

   when dest_clock =>
      nb_char: = length_11 + 2;
      to_be_displayed (1 .. nb_char): = ascii.esc & 'H' & str;
         -- esc'H' positions the cursor on the first line
```

```
            when dest_chrono =>
                nb_char: = length_11 + 3;
                to_be_displayed: = ascii.esc & 'H' & ascii.lf & str;
                    -- esc'H' followed by line feed puts the cursor on the second
                    -- line

            end case;
        end if;
    end loop;
end write;
```

BIBLIOGRAPHY

Here are a few books on the languages Portal, Modula-2 and Ada respectively. In each case they are listed in the order in which the reader is advised to study them, starting with the most general treatments.

PORTAL

BUSINGER, A., *Portal Language Description*, Springer Verlag, 1985.

MODULA-2

WIRTH, N., *Programming in Modula-2*, Springer Verlag (3rd edn), 1985.
THALMANN, D., *Modula-2: An Introduction*, Springer Verlag, 1985.
WIENER, R., FORD, G., *Modula-2: A Software Development Approach*, J. Wiley, 1985.
WIENER, R., SINCOVEC, R., *Software Engineering with Modula-2 and Ada*. J. Wiley, 1984.

ADA

BARNES, J.G.P., *Programming in Ada*, Addison-Wesley, 1984.
GEHANI, N., *Ada Concurrent Programming*, Prentice-Hall, 1984.
BURNS, A., *Concurrent Programming in Ada*, Cambridge University Press, 1985.
BOOCH, G., *Software Engineering with Ada*, Benjamin/Cummins, 1983.
BOOCH, G., *Software Components with Ada*, Benjamin/Cummings, 1987.
BUHR, R.J.A. *System Design with Ada*, Prentice-Hall, 1984.
Le VERRAND, D., *Evaluating Ada*, North Oxford Academic, 1985.

REFERENCES IN THE TEXT

[Barnes 76] J.G.P. BARNES, *RTL/2: Design and Philosophy*, Heyden, London, 1976.

[Brinch Hansen 75] P. BRINCH HANSEN, The Programming Language Concurrent Pascal, *IEEE Trans. on Software Engineering*, SE-1, 2 (June 1975), pp. 199–207.

[Businger 85] A. BUSINGER, *Portal Language Description*, Springer Verlag, 1985.

[Computer 84] Software for Industrial Process Control. *Computer*, 14, 2 (Feb. 84).

[Courtois 71] P.J. COURTOIS, F. HEYMANS, D.L. PARNAS, Concurrent Control with Readers and Writers, *CACM*, 15, 10 (Oct. 71), pp. 667–668.

[DEC 83] *PDP-11 Architecture Handbook*, Digital Equipment Corporation, 1983.

[Dijkstra 68] E.W. DIJKSTRA, Co-operating Sequential Processes, *Programming Languages*, F. Genius (Ed.), Academic Press, pp. 43–112, 1968.

[Dod 83] *Ada Programming Language*, United States Department of Defense, Jan. 83.

[Eventoff 80] W. EVENTOFF, D. HARVEY, R.J. PRICE, The Rendez-vous and Monitor Concepts: Is There an Efficiency Difference?, *ACM SIGPLAN Notices*, 15, 11 (Nov. 80), pp. 156–165.

[Gomaa 84] H. GOMAA, A Software Design Method for Real-Time Systems, *CACM*, 27, 9 (Sept. 84), pp. 938–949.

[Hoare 74] C.A.R. HOARE, Monitors: An Operating System Structuring Concept, *CACM*, 17, 10 (Oct. 74), pp. 549–557.

[Hoare 78] C.A.R. HOARE, Communicating Sequential Processes, *CACM*, 21, 8 (Aug. 78), pp. 666–677.

[Peterson 81] G.L. PETERSON, Myths about the Mutual Exclusion Problem, *Information Processing Letters*, 12, 3 (June 81), pp. 115–116.

[Raynal 84] M. RAYNAL, *Algorithms for Mutual Exclusion*, North Oxford Academic, 1984.

[Robert 77] P. ROBERT, J.P. VERJUS, Towards Autonomous Description of Synchronization Modules, *Proc. IFIP Congress*, North Holland, 1977, pp. 981–986.

[Spector 84] A. SPECTOR, Computer Software for Process Control, *Scientific American*, Sept. 84, pp. 127–138.

[Wirth 77] N. WIRTH, Modula: A Language for Modular Multiprogramming, *Software-Practice and Experience*, 7, 1 (Jan.–Feb. 77), pp. 3–35.

[Wirth 84] N. WIRTH, Revisions and Amendments to Modula-2, *Berichte des Instituts für Informatik*, Nr. 59, ETHZ, June 84.

[Wirth 85] N. WIRTH, *Programming in Modula-2*, Springer Verlag (3rd edn), 1985.

[Woodward 70] P.M. WOODWARD, P.R. WETHERALL, B. GORMAN, *Official Definition of Coral 66*, HMSO, London, 1970.

[Werum 83] W. WERUM, H. WINDAUER, *Introduction to PEARL: process and experiment automation realtime language*, Heyden, 1983.

229

INDEX